e and hope that these people left behind • LA PAZ • We are changed forever • We wil
Everyone has a story Never stop listening • The world is one villag
amazing towers Today I kneel before them and pray • His hopes an
ld with my loved ones • The hole in my heart is still there • Make the lessons of 9/11 ma
share the same pain • Alone we can do little things to change the world and together we
ge • I think in such cases we all should be together to bear such awful grief • But the sp
eaks a little • The shockwaves hit the entire world • I remember how beautiful the sky wa
riends • May we never take life for granted • The silence from their lost lives has had a p
ight It's like a permanent photograph stored in my head reminding me to live each day an
felt the whole world stand still and unified • Peace love joy for all countries • Thank you
s that love and bravery come from • HOPE • Little did I know the towers would be gone in
m courage and forgiveness • PACE • It was in that moment that I became an adult • May
ve since that day embraced a growing responsibility and awareness as a global citizen •
ted to do something to help. • We are all one people• PAIX • What happened on Septembe
lives that are changed in a single moment • What happened here in our country was a trag
arity hope love • One planet one people • We all care • I love NYC • This sorrow should ne
changed forever • We will never forget • HOPE • I can see the love and hope that these pe
g Be courageous • Peace to the victims Respect to the families • Everyone has a story Ne
hy country • Last time I was in New York I stood on top of those amazing towers Today I kn
ay on I promised myself that I would spend as much time as I could with my loved ones •
I will haunt me • The events of 9/11 marked my life forever • We share the same pain • Al
day that changed the world • Let us teach compassion and courage • I think in such cases
ous to see • HOPE • Every time I think of that day my heart breaks a little • The shockwa
only with love • From now on I promise I will help my fellow friends • May we never take
d be grateful for everything we have • I'll never forget that night It's like a permanent ph
a's worst and best hour • A city mourns A city will rebuild • I felt the whole world stand
FDNY you are the best of the best without a doubt • Where does that love and bravery c
11th 2001 all state lines became erased • Peace heroism courage and forgiveness • PAC
est metal in the world the human spirit is • PACE • I have since that day embraced a grow
lieve that there is a lot of good in humanity • We all wanted to do something to help. • We
eace starts from within • I have become more aware of the lives that are changed in a si
The twin towers symbolized the hope of world peace • Solidarity hope love • One planet
ake life for granted • LA PAZ • I sat in silent horror • We are changed forever • We will

September 11, 2001

9/11:
the world speaks

Tribute WTC Visitor Center
A Project of the
September 11th Families' Association
www.tributewtc.org

Lyons Press
Guilford, Connecticut
An imprint of Globe Pequot Press

These voices represent a few of the visitors who have come to
the Tribute WTC Visitor Center over the past five years.

Lyons Press is an imprint of Globe Pequot Press.

Project editors: Lara Asher and Kristen Mellitt
Designer: Diana Nuhn
Layout: Maggie Peterson
Map © Morris Book Publishing, LLC

Grateful acknowledgment to the following for granting permission for use of their artwork:
Peter Arnell: p. 19
George Harkins: pp. 33, 51, 71, 111, 155
Alan Klein: p. ix
Joelle Maslaton: p. 242
Stan Ries: pp. 29, 59, 101, 118-119, 211
"Tiles for America Project," Contemporary Ceramic Studio Association (tiles) and Jack Ader
(photographs): pp. 23, 44, 89, 239
Tribute WTC Visitor Center: p. ix

Library of Congress Cataloging-in-Publication Data is available on file.

ISBN 978-0-7627-7799-0

Printed in the United States of America

10 9 8 7 6 5 4 3 2 1

For all young people worldwide. We can't change what happened
on September 11, 2001, but we can change tomorrow.
Through education and understanding we
can make tomorrow a better day.

Foreword by Mayor Rudolph Giuliani

I am honored to lend my voice to the Tribute Center project. This gives a voice to the thousands of those who visit Ground Zero, the site of a mass murder on American soil.

Since September 11, 2001, I have had the opportunity to travel and discuss this horrible day with both the families of the victims and with world leaders. I have been deeply moved to hear messages of support, anger, loss, fear, and even hope from around the globe. These words have sustained my own sense of purpose over the years and helped remind me that what happened to us in New York City also happened to the world. The world was with us when the Towers fell, and we must keep the memory of that universal feeling of connection and sympathy alive, or this monstrous act will surely be repeated.

On September 11, 2001, the world saw evil incarnate on its television screens. But something else was on display, as well. As firefighters and police rushed in to lead the biggest evacuation in American history, we witnessed incredible courage and selflessness. That inspired our entire country and indeed represented the very first step toward recovery as the terrorists who sought to break our spirit realized we were stronger than anyone realized.

There is a tradition at the Western Wall in Jerusalem for visitors to leave prayers and messages. The Tribute Center has a similar program, and visitors are encouraged to leave notes and artwork about their visit. This book contains examples of the remarkable letters they have shared.

The voices from the postcards left at Ground Zero are unbearably poignant. The letters written by family members are raw with emotion that never fades, even years later. The visitors come from all over the world: A teacher from Singapore writes about how he approaches the lessons of September 11 in the classroom. A man from Thailand sends a message of optimism. One mother mourns her husband with the son who never met his father.

One letter struck a chord within me: "I wasn't ready to say goodbye like that." These simple, powerful words will linger with me. I urge you to read these letters.

Preface by Tom Brokaw

When people ask what has been my most difficult journalistic assignment I don't hesitate.

9/11, the attack on America. It was so unexpected and so violent and so traumatic that the scars will linger for a long, long time.

I went on the air shortly after the airliners hit the Twin Trade Towers and stayed on almost constantly for the next two weeks, morning, noon, and night—trying to keep our audience fully informed about the attack, the consequences, the response of the United States government, and the obligation we all had to each other to get through this together.

On Saturday morning at the end of the first week, I made my way to Ground Zero—I had to see it for myself—and although I have seen more than my share of war's destructive capacity, I was still stunned by the magnitude of the wreckage, the surreal landscape of collapsed buildings, shattered steel and concrete, still smoldering.

How will we get through this, I wondered.

And then I realized where I had gotten my own strength in the preceding week: The American Family, come together once again to face a common assault on all we hold dear, to grieve, to resolve, and to heal.

We were, I think, inspired in ways we could not appreciate at the time by the dignity and the strength of the 9/11 families of the victims—the office workers and bus boys, the firemen and Port Authority workers, the visitors and the long time residents, the airline passengers and crews.

In their grief and in their bewilderment the survivors showed us all the way to another day—and for that I will always be grateful and my admiration knows no bounds.

Introduction

In the early morning of September 11, 2001, I spoke on the phone with my son Jonathan just as his company, Squad 288 Fire Department of New York (FDNY), was leaving to respond to the attack on the World Trade Center. When I realized the magnitude of the event, I rushed into lower Manhattan to lend a hand. Although I was retired from the FDNY, I knew they could use additional assistance considering the unbelievable scale of two fires roaring almost a quarter mile above ground. The moment the Twin Towers collapsed, my mission of trying to help changed into a mission of trying to find my son. It took three months to the day until we found his body. Of course I could not leave the other fathers who were still looking for their sons, and I remained at the site searching for victims until the recovery officially ended in late May 2002.

While I was at the site I was determined to share my story and the stories of what happened to people on September 11th with as many people as I could. At first, I primarily spoke with journalists, but one day I offered to walk a group of high school students around the perimeter of the World Trade Center site. From that moment on, I realized that visitors to the city wanted to hear about people's personal experiences on September 11th and in its aftermath. I recognized that providing accurate information and supporting education were going to be primary tools in this fight against terrorism.

I began meeting with other family groups to discuss common issues, and in 2004 our group, the September 11th Families' Association, moved into an office overlooking the World Trade Center site. Every day my colleague Jennifer Adams and I witnessed thousands of tourists coming to the World Trade Center site to see what transpired or to pay their respects. Realizing that there was nothing here to help them understand, Jennifer proposed the idea of building a center where visitors could meet and listen to the intimate stories of people who directly experienced the attacks. This led to Jennifer and I cofounding the Tribute WTC Visitor Center.

In 2005, we began a walking tour program with remarkable volunteer guides from the 9/11 community who were eager to recount their personal stories. They included family members who

People turned their grief into actions to serve

lost loved ones, survivors who made it out of the buildings, Lower Manhattan residents, FDNY, NYPD, recovery workers, and other volunteers who came to help in the aftermath of 9/11. In September 2006, we opened the Tribute WTC Visitor Center in a small space across the street from the World Trade Center site. We have welcomed millions of visitors from around the world to our five galleries where they learn about the vibrant WTC community prior to September 11th; the attacks of February 26, 1993, and of September 11, 2001; the outpouring of generosity from people across the country and around the world during the recovery; and the victims, those beautiful people who did nothing more than come to work that day.

Before they end their time at the Tribute Center, visitors are offered the opportunity to share their stories and reflections with us on visitor cards. We have collected cards from 200,000 people from 120 countries written in 47 different languages. These cards are remarkable in their overwhelming sentiment about preserving our common humanity.

Everyone is passionate about something. I am passionate about sharing the stories of September 11th and about emphasizing the importance that education plays in making tomorrow a better day for our young. I am grateful to have this opportunity to share some of these poignant visitor cards with you. I hope you will enjoy these heartfelt messages of unity with your family and friends. It is my hope that this collection of individual voices will inspire future generations to work together towards peace.

—*Lee Ielpi*

Please share your thoughts with us:
Share your September 11th story. How have you been changed
by the events of September 11th, or what action can you take
in the spirit of Tribute to help or educate another?

WHY ?

NEWCASTLE. ENGLAND.

United Kingdom

"The shockwaves hit the entire world."

Please share your thoughts with us:
Share your September 11th story. How have you been changed by the events of September 11th, or what action can you take in the spirit of Tribute to help or educate another?

It is hard to find any words to even begin to explain the sorrow Lost dreams Lost anniversaries Lost lives. Few events in our lifetime impacted us a nation like this disaster, and the shockwaves hit the entire world. It miniatured day-to day affairs and brought people together I hope that in years to come the memory stays fresh, the issue-at hand relevant, so that people who do not remember where they were when the attack happened (3rd period biology) will know what happened here.

In prayers,

United States

TRANSLATION

The world changed on 11th of September 2001. The events of that day will be remembered by everyone, forever. It marked the end of an era, but also meant the beginning of a new chapter. A chapter in which peace, freedom, and consensus are most important.

I believe in this. The more people that believe this with me, the faster the chapter will be written.

Please share your thoughts with us:

Share your September 11th story. How have you been changed by the events of September 11th, or what action can you take in the spirit of Tribute to help or educate another?

De wereld veranderde op 11 september 2001 De gebeurtenissen van die dag zullen iedereen bijblyven, voorgoed.

Het markeerde het eind van een tijdperk, maar betekende ook het begin van een nieuw hoofdstuk. Een hoofdstuk waarin vrede, vrijheid en eensgezindheid het belangrijkste zijn

Ik geloof daarin Hoe meer mensen met mij geloven, hoe sneller dat hoofdstuk geschreven zal worden.

1 maart, 2011

The Netherlands

"To this day that phone call will haunt me."

Please share your thoughts with us:
Share your September 11th story. How have you been changed
by the events of September 11th, or what action can you take
in the spirit of Tribute to help or educate another?

I WAS WORKING FOR VIRGIN ATLANTIC AIRWAYS IN THE
UK ON THE DAY TERROR STRUCK IN NEW YORK.
I CAN REMEMBER BEING CALLED TO THE CREW ROOM
& WATCHING THE EVENTS UNFOLD IN HORROR BUT A
EERIE SILENCE

THAT AFTERNOON, I TOOK A CALL FROM A LADY WHOSE
DAUGHTER WORKED ON THE 97TH FLOOR, SHE WAS DESPERATE
TO GET A FLIGHT OUT TO FIND HER DAUGHTER &
TO THIS DAY THAT PHONECALL WILL HAUNT ME, AS I
WILL NEVER KNOW IF SHE MANAGED TO SEE HER
DAUGHTER AGAIN

United Kingdom

"Flaming chunks of steel started to rain down & hit the street."

Please share your thoughts with us:

Share your September 11th story. How have you been changed by the events of September 11th, or what action can you take in the spirit of Tribute to help or educate another?

I was in Tower 1, on the sublevel, B4, working in my office when the lights flickered on & off. None of us knew what had happened & that our lives would forever change from that day forward. Our office blew up around us when the blast from many floors above us traveled down the freight Elevator shaft & into our office. By the grace of God, we made it to street level & thought we were clear of danger when the 2nd plane hit tower 2 just above Vessey st. where I exited the mall. I ran & almost didn't make it across the street when flaming chunks of steel started to rain down & hit the street. I survived by getting under a parked car, came out when the "shower" stopped & ran & never looked back. I am alive today but can't understand why so many friends & collegues arent. I WILL NEVER FORGET. WE MUST NEVER FORGET.

New York

5

Please share your thoughts with us:
Share your September 11th story. How have you been changed by the events of September 11th, or what action can you take in the spirit of Tribute to help or educate another?

Le 11 Septembre 2001, le monde entier a oublié ses religions, ses differences de couleur, ses idées politiques le 11 septembre 2001, le monde entier etait horrifié

de France

France

"All nations united by grief."

Please share your thoughts with us:
Share your September 11th story. How have you been changed by the events of September 11th, or what action can you take in the spirit of Tribute to help or educate another?

September 11th changed the people of my province (Newfoundland and Labrador, CANADA) forever. Planes carrying travellers from all over the world were redirected to our small towns. My fellow Newfoundlanders stepped up and provided food and shelter to the plane loads of people that continued to arrive. We all watched in horror together, Canadian, American, Chinese, Dutch, Italian, all nations united by grief. We are all still praying for those who lost loved ones. xxoo

Canada

"He said, 'I love NY.' I said, 'I do too.'"

Please share your thoughts with us:
Share your September 11th story. How have you been changed by the events of September 11th, or what action can you take in the spirit of Tribute to help or educate another?

I'm an American, but I live in Tokyo, Japan. Because of the time difference, it was around 10-11pm on Sept. 11th in Japan when the towers were hit.

On the morning of Sept. 12th, I commuted to work on the subway. It was quiet. People were stunned. Many people were reading newspapers with pictures of the towers in flames and clouds of dust. The atmosphere was tense with worry, fear, sadness, disbelief.

I looked to my right and saw a businessman in a drab suit but with a flashy/sparkling tie that looked like it was bought in Vegas. It said, "I ♡ NY". I saw the tie and was happy, yet sad. I said, "I like your tie". He said, "I love NY." I said, 'I do too".

Japan

Please share your thoughts with us:
Share your September 11th story. How have you been changed
by the events of September 11th, or what action can you take
in the spirit of Tribute to help or educate another?

Japan

"It was in that moment that I became an adult. Did I want to? No."

Please share your thoughts with us:

Share your September 11th story. How have you been changed by the events of September 11th, or what action can you take in the spirit of Tribute to help or educate another?

It was my first year teaching and I had to stand in front of 30 12 year olds and try to explain what was happening. it was in that moment that I became an adult. Did I want to? No. I wanted someone to hold me and tell me everything would be alright. But it was my turn to do the holding. I had to reassure and discuss, educate and show these kids that people are stronger when they stand together. The only thing I can do is take the lesson and teach it over and over until its no longer a lesson, but a natural response. Be good to each other because when all is said and done, life is about people.

Philadel

Pennsylvania

"I grew up that day making a promise to myself."

Please share your thoughts with us:
Share your September 11th story. How have you been changed by the events of September 11th, or what action can you take in the spirit of Tribute to help or educate another?

I was in 8th grade when these tragic events occured My study hall teacher wasn't in his classroom At about 9:15 he walked in. He proceeded to ask if any of knew what the WTC or Twin Towers were. Then he told us there were airplanes that struck the towers. I knew we were never going to be the same again I grew up that day making a promise to myself to do what I can and remember the day It had been about 3 years prior when I saw the towers from the Jersey shore I donated any money I could to relief efforts My heart + soul go out to the families of the unsung heroes.

Pennsylvania

TRANSLATION

On 9/11 my nephew called and told me to turn on the television. The previous day I had returned with my husband from New York where we had gone on vacation. I couldn't believe my eyes. What had happened was unbelievably tragic. So many innocents. Why? Why? Why? What did they do? So many mothers, so many orphaned children. Why? Why? Why? Today is 2/8/07 and we came with our children to visit here again, and I have the same questions. It is outside of any logic. Even those who planned this couldn't have imagined something like this would happen. . . .

Please share your thoughts with us:

Share your September 11th story. How have you been changed by the events of September 11th, or what action can you take in the spirit of Tribute to help or educate another?

Στις 9/11 ο ανυψιός μου, με πήρε τηλέφωνο κ' μου είπε ν' ανοίξω την τηλεόραση. Την προηγούμενη μέρα είχα επιστρέψει με τον άντρα μου από την Ν.Υ που είχαμε πάει διακοπές. Δεν πίστευα στα μάτια μου. Αυτό που έγινε ήταν κάτι το αούλητο Τραγικό! Τόσοι αθώοι Γιατι;;; Τι έφταιξαν;; Τόσες Μανάδες, τόσα παιδιά ορφανά Γιατι;; Σήμερα 2/8/2007 ήρθαμε με τα παιδιά μας και πάλι. Έχω τα ίδια ερωτήματα Είναι έξω από κάθε λογική Ούτε αυτοί πάντο σχεδίασαν θα είχαν φανταστεί κάτι τέτοιο. Εύχομαι ειρήνη κ' λογική να επικρατήσει σε όλο τον κόσμο.

Greece

TRANSLATION

The 9/11 tragedy is a story in the lives of all people in our world. This will change our perspective on the importance of life itself. I hope we will be more sensitive, be more loving and responsible people. Life on earth is short. Let's give importance to it.

Please share your thoughts with us:
Share your September 11th story. How have you been changed by the events of September 11th, or what action can you take in the spirit of Tribute to help or educate another?

Ang 9/11 na kwento ay kwento ng buhay ng lahat ng tao sa mundo. Ito ay nakapag-pabago sa pananaw sa kahalagahan ng buhay ng tao. Sana tayo ay mas maging sensitibo, mapagpahalaga sa ibang tao at mapagmahal. Ang buhay sa mundo ay sadyang ~~maigsi~~ maiksi. Bigyan natin ng kahalagahan ito.

Angeles City,
Philippines

Philippines

"What I saw will stay with me forever."

Please share your thoughts with us:
Share your September 11th story. How have you been changed
by the events of September 11th, or what action can you take
in the spirit of Tribute to help or educate another?

I was a news producer for ITN in London.
I had just got married 9/08/01 and 9/11
was my first day back at work. I saw the planes
go into the WTC and alerted my editor - from
then on it was over to rolling news. I was
a chief-sub who had to log all the footage
that came in - What I saw will stay with
me forever - especially those souls who felt
they had no option but to jump. I still see
their faces - still have nightmares - still in Therapy.

United Kingdom

Please share your thoughts with us:
Share your September 11th story. How have you been changed by the events of September 11th, or what action can you take in the spirit of Tribute to help or educate another?

Tribute WTC 9/11 · Person to Person History ·

Israel

"His hopes and dreams live on in his two wonderful children."

As a fresh MBA graduate my husband, Joseph, started his first business venture at No 1 WTC. Many years later, he took me on our first date to the Windows of the World.

And on September 11, 2001, he lost his life at the Windows of the World, in the WTC — one of his favorite places!

His hopes and dreams live on in his two wonderful children.

Massachusetts

Please share your thoughts with us:
Share your September 11th story. How have you been changed by the events of September 11th, or what action can you take in the spirit of Tribute to help or educate another?

Tribute WTC 9/11 · Person to Person History ·

WE ALL CARE

New York

"'If you want them to come for you, you have to go for them.'"

Please share your thoughts with us:
Share your September 11th story. How have you been changed by the events of September 11th, or what action can you take in the spirit of Tribute to help or educate another?

A fire fighter, when asked how he could run into a burning building, said "If you want them to come for you, you have to go for them."

If ever you will want someone to come for you - when you have fallen, or are lost, or sick, or poor - you have to go for them <u>Now</u>

St. Paul, Minnesota

Minnesota

TRANSLATION

We, the former firefighters of Vietnam, admire the courage and sacrifice of the firefighters of New York who have saved thousands of people in the two towers. When the people were trying to run out and escape, you are the people who ran in. This is the beautiful ethic of firefighters.

On behalf of the firefighters of the former South Vietnam, the former head of the firefighters' department in South Vietnam

Please share your thoughts with us:

Share your September 11th story. How have you been changed by the events of September 11th, or what action can you take in the spirit of Tribute to help or educate another?

Chúng tôi, những cán bộ chiến sỹ Lực lượng Cảnh sát Phòng cháy và chữa cháy Việt Nam vô cùng cảm kích trước sự dũng cảm, hy sinh của những người chữa cháy New York, nhờ đó đã cứu thoát hàng vạn người ở 2 tòa tháp. Trong lúc mọi người tìm cách để thoát ra thì các người đồng nghiệp chữa cháy đã xông vào! Đó là ý chí cao đẹp của người lính chữa cháy!

28/9/2008   Thay mặt Lực lượng Cảnh sát PCC Việt Nam

Cục trưởng Cục Cảnh sát PCCC VN.

Vietnam

"I thank God that New York was strong enough to weather the storm."

Please share your thoughts with us:
Share your September 11th story. How have you been changed
by the events of September 11th, or what action can you take
in the spirit of Tribute to help or educate another?

I was on a ship in the US Navy on 9/11. I had only visited NYC for the
first time a few months ago, and I didn't make it to the Towers; I assumed
I'd get another chance. In January 2002 my ship visited New Jersey and
I took a ferry to Manhattan. I had to see what was left. When I thought
about the trajedy I remembered people I lost that day, and all the other
people who lost people they love. I'm here today because my current ship
is visiting for Fleet Week, and of all the tourist sites to visit in NYC,
there was no choice more important to me than revisiting this site. I'm
not angry, but I am still horrified by the intensity of this attack, and
I'm a little surprised that it still hurts so much 8 years later. I thank
God that New York was strong enough to weather the storm, but concerned
enough never to forget or take her heroes for granted. I thank the
people responsible for this memorial, and the thousands who come to see
and keep our hopes alive. God bless.

20 MAY 09

USS IWO JIMA (LHD7)

United States

21

"Thank you for holding the flame."

Please share your thoughts with us:
Share your September 11th story. How have you been changed by the events of September 11th, or what action can you take in the spirit of Tribute to help or educate another?

There were The Years prior To 9/11/2001, and all The Years since. Two distinct chapters in American life. World life? Probably. Thank You for holding The flame.

Arizona

"I still carry it."

Please share your thoughts with us:
Share your September 11th story. How have you been changed
by the events of September 11th, or what action can you take
in the spirit of Tribute to help or educate another?

9/11 was my first day at
college My college ID shows the
date so I still carry it in my
purse

Ireland

Ireland

"Let us teach compassion and courage."

Please share your thoughts with us:
Share your September 11th story. How have you been changed by the events of September 11th, or what action can you take in the spirit of Tribute to help or educate another?

ST. PETER'S SCHOOL, BOURNEMOUTH, U.K.

We, as educators, must not strive to create intellectuals who do not know what it is to be a 'citizen'. Let us teach compassion and courage, not conflict + qualification

United Kingdom

TRANSLATION

It seems to us that we have achieved everything that was possible to achieve. Technology, science, the whole civilization has accelerated our pulse to such a degree that life resembles a thought that passes very quickly. Let's remember however that such mechanical life of human beings should not be devoid of human impulses.

Please share your thoughts with us:

Share your September 11th story. How have you been changed by the events of September 11th, or what action can you take in the spirit of Tribute to help or educate another?

Wydaje nam się, że osiągnęliśmy wszystko co tylko można było. Technika, nauka, całe cywilizacja przyspieszają nane tętna do tego stopnia, iż życie przypomina myśl, która bardzo szybko przemija. Pamiętajmy jednak, że to mechaniczne życie człowieka nie pomimo być pozbawione ludzkich odruchów.

We are all humans being, We all have right to live. Do not forget about love to other people. We have only one world to share!

Poland

"We are all part of humanity."

Please share your thoughts with us:
Share your September 11th story. How have you been changed by the events of September 11th, or what action can you take in the spirit of Tribute to help or educate another?

I'm from Panama, but we have always had a close link to the U.S. because of the Panama Canal. When the events of 9-11 took place I was in my College's cafeteria and not even a single person returned to class.
We may belong to different countries, but are events like this that touch our hearts and make us remember we are all part of humanity.
My deepest condolence to those who lost their loved ones and may them rest in peace.
May something like this never take place again.

Panama

"I grew up in the shadow of the towers, I miss them still."

Please share your thoughts with us:
Share your September 11th story. How have you been changed by the events of September 11th, or what action can you take in the spirit of Tribute to help or educate another?

I was living and working in the former Yugoslavia on Sept 11. I watched this terrible event on TV, like so many Americans abroad, we were determined to get home but helpless to do so. Never in my life had I ever felt so much rage and love at the same time. I grew up in the shadow of the towers, I miss them still.

Florida

28

On our first visit to NY we visited the Twin Towers. It was one of the most emblematic places in the city. In our videotape of 9/11/1991, exactly 10 years before they were destroyed, we were able to admire them and contemplate their magnificent views from high above. This is a true tragedy. The worst part is the many lives lost. There is no justification, there never will be. We are very sorry, with all our heart, our memories and sorrow for what took place.

Please share your thoughts with us:
Share your September 11th story. How have you been changed by the events of September 11th, or what action can you take in the spirit of Tribute to help or educate another?

15-10-2008

En nuestro primer viaje a N.York visitamos las torres Gemelas. Era uno de los lugares mas emblemáticos de la ciudad. En nuestra cinta video 11-09-1991, justo diez años antes de ser destruidas, las pudimos admirar i contemplar sus magníficas vistas desde lo alto. Es una verdadera tragedia. Lo peor es las vidas que la misma costó. No hay justificación, nunca la habrá. Lo sentimos muchísimo, con todo nuestro corazón, nuestro recuerdo y sentimiento por lo ocurrido.
Desde Palamós (GIRONA) ESPAÑA

Spain

TRANSLATION

. . . The fragmented words, sentences, and images still have the power to shock—and leave tears streaming uncontrollably down the face. Even if history's river will eventually wash away the past, our memories will still be fresh and never fade away. . . . This is not only to say that whatever is lost will never be recovered, but also more about the lessons learned so that history will not repeat itself. After experiencing the 5/12 earthquake in China, this feeling resonates even more deeply with me. I wish for world peace; peace in the sense that it isn't only about eliminating wars.

Please share your thoughts with us:
Share your September 11th story. How have you been changed by the events of September 11th, or what action can you take in the spirit of Tribute to help or educate another?

令我感叹的是，七年之后，这个博物馆依然，访客络绎不绝。那些只言片语和画面依然有震撼人心的力量，令人泪流满面。尽管历史的长河会无尽地冲刷，但有些记忆会始终鲜明，不曾滚去。能够做到这点，依靠的不仅是事件本身的严重程度，更多的是人们从中得到了什么，学会了什么 Nothing will ever be the same，不仅说的是那些失去的永远不可返得，更是说人们会吸取教训让历史不再重演 此时，在经历了中国今年5 12大地震之后，这种感触更深

愿世界和平，而和平，不仅是消灭战争吧

China

31

"My backyard was littered with burnt pieces of paper."

Please share your thoughts with us:
Share your September 11th story. How have you been changed
by the events of September 11th, or what action can you take
in the spirit of Tribute to help or educate another?

I live 12 miles away
from WTC. Next morning
my backyard was littered
with Burnt pieces of paper
that the wind blew
It was almost like the souls of
the people who just died came

New York

Broadway night September 2001,

"I think back on September 11, 2001."

Please share your thoughts with us:
Share your September 11th story. How have you been changed by the events of September 11th, or what action can you take in the spirit of Tribute to help or educate another?

I first visited NYC the weekend prior to 911. I remember looking at the WTC in awe. The morning of the attacks a friend who lived in the city called my apartment screaming on the answering machine. My roommates & I turned on the TV to witness the scene. A month after the attacks I dropped out of my Junior year at college to join the military. Six ½ years later I'm on my 2nd enlistment and been to Iraq twice. When asked how do I put up with the tempo & deployments of the military I think back on September 11, 2001. My brothers and sisters in arms would much rather take the fight to them then allow terrorists to hit our home again.

— A 9·11 Soldier/Proud to Serve
31 Dec 08

I WILL NEVER FORGET

Georgia

34

TRANSLATION

On September 11, 2001, I was 11 years old. I was returning from school because in our country, in Switzerland, it was 4 o'clock in the afternoon. My mother was sitting in front of the TV, I sat down to see. I thought at first that this was a film, then my mother explained to me that no, this was very much reality. . . . I stayed all night in front of the TV because I couldn't believe it. RIP to all of the people who died and courage to their loved ones. Let us put an end to terrorism. A thought from a Swiss woman.

Please share your thoughts with us:
Share your September 11th story. How have you been changed by the events of September 11th, or what action can you take in the spirit of Tribute to help or educate another?

Le 11 septembre 2001 j'avais 11 ans. Je rentrais de l'école car chez nous, en suisse il était 16h de l'après-midi. Ma maman repassait devant la TV et je m'assis pour regarder. Je pensais tout d'abord, que c'était un film, puis ma mère m'expliqua que non c'était bien la réalité. . . . Je restai toute la nuit devant la TV car je n'y croyais pas. Rip à toutes les personnes qui sont décédées et courage à leurs proches. Mettons fin au terrorisme !

Une pensée depuis la Suisse

Switzerland

"My mother pressed a tissue to her mouth to muffle her sobs."

Please share your thoughts with us:
Share your September 11th story. How have you been changed by the events of September 11th, or what action can you take in the spirit of Tribute to help or educate another?

I remember coming downstairs the morning of the attack. My parents were watching the news, watching that tape of the towers collapsing playing over and over again. My mother pressed a tissue to her mouth to muffle her sobs while my father held his head in his hands. I asked them what was going on — it was strange that they were watching TV on a school morning. My mother shushed me and whispered, "Something terrible has happened". I was 7 years old.

California

"Today, I realize, we have to remember it."

Please share your thoughts with us:
Share your September 11th story. How have you been changed by the events of September 11th, or what action can you take in the spirit of Tribute to help or educate another?

On Septembe 11th, 2001 , I saw that on TV in korea at that time I was shocked even if I was child and I lived in korea

Today, I realize, We have to remember it peace ♪

South Korea

TRANSLATION

On the morning of September 11, my mother called me to tell me that "a plane had crashed against the WTC." When I saw what had taken place I could only think it was another big accident, like what happened with the "Challenger" years before; I never thought this would be a new day that would separate our history into before and after. . . .

Hate can knock down buildings and people, but love can build new worlds and give them life.

Please share your thoughts with us:
Share your September 11th story. How have you been changed by the events of September 11th, or what action can you take in the spirit of Tribute to help or educate another?

EN LA MAÑANA DEL 11 SEPT DE 2001, MI MADRE ME LLAMÓ DICIENDO "UN AVIÓN CHOCO EL WTC", Y AL VER LO QUE HABÍA SUCEDIDO, SÓLO PENSÉ QUE SERÍA UN GRAN ACCIDENTE MÁS, COMO LO SUCEDIDO CON EL "CHALENGER" AÑOS ATRÁS, JAMÁS PENSÉ QUE ESTO SERÍA UN NUEVO DÍA CERO QUE SEPARARÍA NUESTRA HISTORIA EN UN ANTES Y DESPUÉS....

EL ODIO PUEDE HABER DERRIBADO EDIFICIOS Y GENTE, PERO EL AMOR PUEDE CONSTRUIR NUEVOS MUNDOS Y DARLES VIDA.

CHILE.

Chile

Please share your thoughts with us:
Share your September 11th story. How have you been changed by the events of September 11th, or what action can you take in the spirit of Tribute to help or educate another?

I'll protect you.
There won't be anymore disaster.

South Korea

"My mom . . . knew she had to become a police officer."

Please share your thoughts with us:
Share your September 11th story. How have you been changed by the events of September 11th, or what action can you take in the spirit of Tribute to help or educate another?

September 11th really shook my family hard. Though I was young when it happened I know the importance of this event and I will hold it in my heart for as long as I live Although there were many bad things came out of that day, there was one brave person that emerged from my family and that was my mom She knew she had to become a police officer to protect and member 9/11 . but let it never happen again

California

TRANSLATION

When 9/11 happened, I was in the military. Although I was very upset at that time, I didn't really have any other feelings. Six years later, it is my first time visiting NY. Coming to see Ground Zero gave me a strong shocking feeling. When I watched all these documentaries and photographs, I could not help crying. When I saw these images one by one and recalled every single moment that happened at that time, all is a tragedy. Everyone who was shocked, every family that was broken. We are One World. I will do my best to make it better.

Please share your thoughts with us:
Share your September 11th story. How have you been changed by the events of September 11th, or what action can you take in the spirit of Tribute to help or educate another?

911發生的時侯,我正在當兵.當時對於這樣的事件,雖然覺得難過憤怒,可是也沒有特別其他的感覺,事隔6年多第一次來到NY觀光,來參觀 Ground Zero,有一股很強烈的振憾,看到這些紀錄片&照片,不禁使我濕了双眼.看到這一幕幕的影像,再回想當初發生時的情況,每一個驚恐的人,每一個破碎的家庭,都是一場悲劇.世界是一個共同体,我當盡力去使它更好

MAR. 20.

Taiwan

41

"How everyone reacted, is our legacy."

Please share your thoughts with us:
Share your September 11th story. How have you been changed by the events of September 11th, or what action can you take in the spirit of Tribute to help or educate another?

I come from Alpine Utah. A small city in comparison with the "big apple". Still, as I walk down these streets, through these memorials, and past these people, I am astounded by the incredible courage and faith all around me. What happened here, in our country, was a tragedy. How everyone reacted, is our legacy. May this courage never die.

Utah

TRANSLATION

September 11th will always be marked in my generation's memory as the most inhumane act that was ever committed. I watched at home, incredulously, what was about to happen on the other side of the ocean and never again looked at the world in the same way. I cried for those who died, but I also cried because I realized that, in the midst of so much pain and loss, people united and showed the attackers that that was not the end; it was the beginning of a fight for peace and tolerance.

Please share your thoughts with us:

Share your September 11th story. How have you been changed by the events of September 11th, or what action can you take in the spirit of Tribute to help or educate another?

O 11 de Setembro ficará para sempre marcado na memória de minha geração como o mais desumano acto que alguém cometeu. Assisti em casa, incrédula, ao que que estava a passar do outro lado do oceano e nunca mais olhei para o mundo da mesma maneira. Chorei pelos que morreram, mas chorei também porque percebi que, no meio de tanta dor e perda, o ser humano uniu-se e mostrou aos atacantes que aquele não era o fim, mas uma mina de uma luta pela paz e tolerância.

Portugal

ASIAN AMERICAN
LATIN AMERICAN
AFRO AMERICAN
AMERICAN
ITALIAN AMERICAN
ARAB AMERICAN
GERMAN AMERICAN
NATIVE AMERICAN
IRISH AMERICAN
UNIDOS
THE
REMEMBERS

"We are the memories. We are the hope. We are tomorrow."

Please share your thoughts with us:
Share your September 11th story. How have you been changed
by the events of September 11th, or what action can you take
in the spirit of Tribute to help or educate another?

Before that day there was you and me, them and us.
We were a people divided, a nation divided, a country
and world and universe divided. We cannot keep
pointing the fingers. We move on. We are the
memories. We are the hope. We are tomorrow.

Washington

"Lives that are changed in a single moment."

Please share your thoughts with us:
Share your September 11th story. How have you been changed
by the events of September 11th, or what action can you take
in the spirit of Tribute to help or educate another?

I have spent the last 4 summers working with the children of Sept. 11. It has made that day so real to me. To see how the lives of these children were changed. They are the strongest people I know. I have seen them start HS. and this year many of them are now in their first year of university.

I view the world differently now. I used to be very jaded and removed from what was happening in the world around me. The war, an earthquake, a bomb. These happened millions of miles (or so it seemed) away and did not affect me. I have become more aware of the lives that are changed in a single moment.

My mission is to make everyone else more aware of their global village. A life is a life, no matter where. They should not be just another news story.

Canada

Please share your thoughts with us:

Share your September 11th story. How have you been changed by the events of September 11th, or what action can you take in the spirit of Tribute to help or educate another?

Tribute WTC 9/11 · Person to Person History ·

I was born 2 months after my Dad died on 9/11 and I miss him a lot

DAD

I ♡ NY

United Kingdom

Please share your thoughts with us:
Share your September 11th story. How have you been changed by the events of September 11th, or what action can you take in the spirit of Tribute to help or educate another?

Portugal

TRANSLATION

. . . I was at the Price Waterhouse Coopers office in Shanghai watching the news on CNN. I could not believe my eyes; I could not believe that humans could be so ruthless. It is absolutely inhumane to use our own hands to wipe out our own kind! . . . I know that human nature is good on the inside. Kindness and hope shall overcome everything. This kind of difficulty can only allow us to emerge even stronger, united and unwavering. Let freedom for the people and faith in democracy prosper!

Please share your thoughts with us:

Share your September 11th story. How have you been changed by the events of September 11th, or what action can you take in the spirit of Tribute to help or educate another?

9/11发生当天 我正坐在上海 Pricewaterhousecoopers 的办公室里看着CNN 的新闻. 我无法相信自己的眼睛, 无法相信人类可以如此疯狂. 残酷 毫无人性的利用自己的双手去毁灭我们自己!

2008年的12月24日圣诞节前夜日. 我来到 Ground Zero. 亲眼看到了这个曾经 被毁为平地的地方, 又开始动工建筑新的 building 看到 威平上还在那场 悲剧中表失掉命以的照比 看到很多人留言. 我知道, 在人类的内心深处 的正, 善良和希望 没有任何东西可以摧毁的! 这样的灾难只能 让我们更加坚强 更加团结 更加坚定 自由民生和政的信念!!!

Florida

Please share your thoughts with us:
Share your September 11th story. How have you been changed
by the events of September 11th, or what action can you take
in the spirit of Tribute to help or educate another?

what can I do?

Japan

Scouts on Church Street 9-'01

"Even though I was only 10 years old I helped make a difference."

Please share your thoughts with us:
Share your September 11th story. How have you been changed by the events of September 11th, or what action can you take in the spirit of Tribute to help or educate another?

When 9/11 happened I was in 5th grade. I was young at the time but I knew I had to help. I had a lemonade stand & instead of charging people I took only donations. Throught the day all the kids in the neighborhood joined me. We raised a total of $8000! Even though I was only 10yrs old I helped make a difference. I Love my country! ♡ ♡

(Illinois)

Illinois

"Education is key!"

Please share your thoughts with us:
Share your September 11th story. How have you been changed
by the events of September 11th, or what action can you take
in the spirit of Tribute to help or educate another?

Education is key!
    and
Respect for others!

C→care for everybody and everything
A→appreciate everybody and everything
R→respect everybody and everything
E→educate everybody.
This is our school moto

CP school – WITNEY
OX FORDSHIRE

United Kingdom

"Where does that love and bravery come from?"

Please share your thoughts with us:
Share your September 11th story. How have you been changed by the events of September 11th, or what action can you take in the spirit of Tribute to help or educate another?

What causes a person to voluntarily rush into a burning building ready to collapse, in hopes of saving lives at great risk to themselves?

Where does that love and bravery come from?

Anonymous

Please share your thoughts with us:
Share your September 11th story. How have you been changed by the events of September 11th, or what action can you take in the spirit of Tribute to help or educate another?

No man's ideology is worth another man's life.

SLEEP WELL MY BROTHERS

Anonymous

"How short, precious, and tragic life can be."

Please share your thoughts with us:
Share your September 11th story. How have you been changed by the events of September 11th, or what action can you take in the spirit of Tribute to help or educate another?

I HAD WORKED NEAR THE WTC, CAME AND WENT FROM THE PATH TRAINS BELOW, AND ALTHOUGH I DID NOT KNOW ANY OF THE VICTIMS PERSONALLY, I WALKED AMONG THEM EVERY DAY.... AND WHEN I COME HERE NOW, I WALK AMONG THEIR SPIRITS... THESE PEOPLE WERE HUMAN BEINGS, JUST LIKE US. EVERYTHING THEY HAD, THEY WERE, WAS GONE.
    I HOPE WHAT WE <u>REALLY</u> NEVER FORGET IS HOW SHORT, PRECIOUS, AND TRAGIC LIFE CAN BE, AND WHAT HATE AND MISGUIDENESS CAN LEAD TO. GOD BLESS THE FALLEN, GOD BLESS US ALL.

MONMOUTH COUNTY, NEW JERSEY

New Jersey

TRANSLATION

Treasure Peace

Hold Hands and Go Forward

Love Life

Enjoy Freedom

Please share your thoughts with us:
Share your September 11th story. How have you been changed by the events of September 11th, or what action can you take in the spirit of Tribute to help or educate another?

珍惜和平

携手进步

热爱生活

享有自由

China

"Little did I know the towers would be gone in my lifetime."

Please share your thoughts with us:
Share your September 11th story. How have you been changed
by the events of September 11th, or what action can you take
in the spirit of Tribute to help or educate another?

I GREW UP ON THE LOWER EAST SIDE JUST A
FEW SHORT BLOCKS FROM THE WTC. I REMEMBER THE OLD
ELECTRONICS SHOPS AND DIGBY'S DEPT STORE THAT WERE
RAZED IN ORDER TO BEGIN THE SUBSTRUCTURE OF THE TOWERS.

YEARS LATER I TOOK MY TWO DAUGHTERS AND A RELATIVE
FROM IRELAND TO THE TOWERS AND OBSERVATION DECK

LITTLE DID I KNOW THE TOWERS WOULD BE GONE IN MY
LIFETIME. MY YOUNGEST DAUGHTER HAS BEEN SO MOVED BY 9-11
THAT SHE HAS WRITTEN SEVERAL SHORT STORIES ABOUT THE
TOWERS AS A FORMER FIGHTER/CHIEF THE LOSS OF SO
MANY BRAVE FIREFIGHTERS ON 9-11 WILL ALWAYS HAUNT ME.

New Jersey

"Life in this world could and would never be the same again."

Tribute WTC 9/11 · Person to Person History

Please share your thoughts with us:
Share your September 11th story. How have you been changed by the events of September 11th, or what action can you take in the spirit of Tribute to help or educate another?

October 10, 2008

When the news of 9-11 struck, the whole world kept its breath!
Everyone realised, that life in this world could and would never be the same again.
Now, 7 years later, the pictures of the suffering, the pain and the sorrow brought tears to my eyes again.
But also did the images of the heroism and the voluntary aid of so many
A monument! Lest we forget!

Holland

The Netherlands

Life in Germany was also changed through 9/11. People mistrust and discriminate against Muslims because of the fear of being attacked. This isn't good. I would like to keep being open-minded. I don't want to be intimidated, and I would like to keep traveling. For me, the most important thing is that 9/11 should not change us, that we can keep trusting each other, and not see a potential criminal in every person.

Please share your thoughts with us:
Share your September 11th story. How have you been changed by the events of September 11th, or what action can you take in the spirit of Tribute to help or educate another?

Auch das Leben in Deutschland hat sich durch „9/11" verändert. Wir haben Furcht vor Anschlägen, oft de mißtraut man Menschen diskriminiert sie, weil sie Moslems sind. Das ist nicht gut.
Ich möchte weiter offen sein, möchte mich nicht ~~vor~~ einschüchtern lassen, möchte auch weiter reisen.
Für mich ist am wichtigsten, dass „9/11" uns nicht verändert, dass wir einander weiter vertrauen, nicht in jedem einen potentiellen Verbrecher sehen!

Germany

"There is a lot of good will in America."

Please share your thoughts with us:
Share your September 11th story. How have you been changed by the events of September 11th, or what action can you take in the spirit of Tribute to help or educate another?

I am a muslim from the united kingdom and what I cant understand is How someone can misuse religion to agress violence. I was 12 years old when thist took place, did not understand it then what had happened But i do now. There is a lot of good will in America and if we can still stick togethe after this we can make it through anything.

United Kingdom

"Let it be no more."

Please share your thoughts with us:
Share your September 11th story. How have you been changed
by the events of September 11th, or what action can you take
in the spirit of Tribute to help or educate another?

เคยมีคนบอกว่าวงจรทำร้ายกัน ของคนไม่เคยจบสิ้น แต่ถ้ามันเป็น วงกลมบ่อยครั้ง
เข้า จะมีรูปแบบเปลี่ยน แล้วมันจะไม่เป็น วงกลมวงกลมอีกต่อไป ขอให้ 9/11 เป็นครั้งสุดท้าย
ที่คนจะร้ายกันฆ่ากัน ตายนับร้อยคน ขอให้ไม่มีอีกเลย
ขอให้ทุกคนที่เสียชีวิตหลับอย่างสงบสุข

A saying goes that the circle of human inflicting pain on each other
never ends, but another saying goes that if a circle repeats itself enough,
an abnormality will occur, and the pattern will break, and the circle will be
no more. Let 9/11 be the last time of this circle that tries to hurt thousands
of People at a time. Let it be no more.
May the dead rest in peace.

Thailand

"Practice tolerance."

Please share your thoughts with us:
Share your September 11th story. How have you been changed
by the events of September 11th, or what action can you take
in the spirit of Tribute to help or educate another?

"P" PRACTICE TOLERANCE

"E" EDUCATE THE PEOPLE ABOUT
CULTURES

"A" ACTIVELY REFUSE FRIENDSHIP
OF ALL

"C" CARESS THE LOVING NATURE
OF THAT THIS WORLD IS
ABOUT

"E" ELIMINATE FROM OUR
LANGUAGES THE WORD
HATE

All People are Made
of Flesh & Blood not
Colour & Religion

Be as one with People
& Nature

An Australian
Police Officer.

Australia

64

Please share your thoughts with us:

Share your September 11th story. How have you been changed by the events of September 11th, or what action can vou take in the spirit of Tribute to help or educate another?

Germany

TRANSLATION

Dear David,

Today we remember you on your tragic departure. We know that it was not in vain because thanks to this sacrifice today we understand and we are convinced that in this world the only thing that will bring tranquility in our lives is to live in peace and love with all other human beings. We remember you with lots of love—your wife and family.

Please share your thoughts with us:
Share your September 11th story. How have you been changed by the events of September 11th, or what action can you take in the spirit of Tribute to help or educate another?

QUERIDO DAVID:

HOY TE RECORDAMOS EN TU TRAGICA PARTIDA, Y SABEMOS QUE NO FUE ENVANO PORQUE GRACIAS A ESTE SACRIFICIO HOY ENTENDEMOS Y ESTAMOS CONVENCIDOS, QUE EN ESTE MUNDO LO UNICO QUE NOS DARÁ TRANQUILIDAD EN NUESTRA VIDA, ES VIVIR EN PAZ Y AMOR ENTRE TODOS LOS SERES HUMANOS.

TE RECUERDA CON MUCHO AMOR TU ESPOSA.

New York

"As a physician, September 11, 2001, inspired me to learn more about trauma care."

Please share your thoughts with us:
Share your September 11th story. How have you been changed by the events of September 11th, or what action can you take in the spirit of Tribute to help or educate another?

As a physician, September 11, 2001 inspired me to learn more about trauma care, mass casualty work, CBRNE agents. As a mother, the day inspired me to hold my children close. As the sister of a firefighter, I became more appreciative. As an American, I learned more about sacrifice.

Alabama

"I am proud to serve this country and protect it."

Please share your thoughts with us:
Share your September 11th story. How have you been changed
by the events of September 11th, or what action can you take
in the spirit of Tribute to help or educate another?

Since 9/11 I have looked at life in a totally different way. It has made me want to join the military. I am proud to serve this country and protect it any way possible. I Love the U.S.A and everyone in it!!

God Bless

Pennsylvania

"These were regular people . . . just going about their day."

I remember the day 6½ years ago. I am Australian... this is my first time to NY, and to the WTC site. Before this visit, I couldn't comprehend the magnitude of the situation... it was images on TV, photos... but now, I have made the connection... These were regular people with a home, some with families, just going about their day. The survivors lives' have changed forever...

However, it is in times like this, TOLERANCE is of such great importance. Society has changed since 9/11, even in Australia. Increased security, increased suspicion, increased racism towards Muslims. A tragic aftermath. This was the act of extremists. It is not the Muslim faith. Peace begins with education and understanding. Let this be the beginning... one planet.

Australia

"Nightly candlelight vigils were held."

Please share your thoughts with us:
Share your September 11th story. How have you been changed by the events of September 11th, or what action can you take in the spirit of Tribute to help or educate another?

My heart was broken on September 11th when so many innocent lives were lost and their voices no longer heard. The silence from their lost lives has had a profound effect on me. Nightly candlelight vigils were held at my dinner table with my children.

Rhode Island

We ate together, nights

Duane Street, September '01, Pot Luck

"I am alive because of 9/11."

Please share your thoughts with us:
Share your September 11th story. How have you been changed by the events of September 11th, or what action can you take in the spirit of Tribute to help or educate another?

I am alive because of 9/11. My Father was one of the rescue workers that responded to the twin towers. He was hurt really bad. Once he got better he decided to have me + my brother

New Jersey

"9/11 inspired me to follow in my father's footsteps."

Please share your thoughts with us:
Share your September 11th story. How have you been changed by the events of September 11th, or what action can you take in the spirit of Tribute to help or educate another?

9-11 inspired me to follow in my father's footsteps and become a firefighter/EMT.

Vermont

TRANSLATION

I want to give condolences to the families of 9/11. Terrorist acts are not a solution to our problems. We are sorry to see that terrorist acts kill people every day. I invite all the college students, Arab and American, to work together to make our world a better place to live and to prevent any terrorist attacks. Even though I know English, I'm writing this in Arabic to show that we have solidarity and sympathy with the victims, their families, and their beloved ones.

Peace-Peace-Peace

Please share your thoughts with us:
Share your September 11th story. How have you been changed by the events of September 11th, or what action can you take in the spirit of Tribute to help or educate another?

أود أن أتقدم بأحر التعازي لأهالي المفقودين. العنف والضغينة لم يكونا يوماً حلاً لمشاكلنا ومن المؤسف أن نرى نتائج العنف تتجسد يومياً بفقدان الأرواح والعقول النيّرة.

أدعو جميع الطلاب والطالبات، العرب والأمريكان إلى التسامح والمحبة والتعاون على جعل عالمنا مكاناً أفضل للعيش، خالٍ من أيّة محاولات إرهابية وإجرامية، مهما كانت!

السلام - السلام - السلام

Lebanon

74

"I wish you could be here."

Please share your thoughts with us:
Share your September 11th story. How have you been changed
by the events of September 11th, or what action can you take
in the spirit of Tribute to help or educate another?

Dear grandPa
I wish you could be here but you
are in heavin I am doing very good
how are you doing?
love
~~the~~ the famly
ps the mets are in first place

New York

"2 eyes to see a new world."

Please share your thoughts with us:
Share your September 11th story. How have you been changed
by the events of September 11th, or what action can you take
in the spirit of Tribute to help or educate another?

WTC

11 Settembre 2001 → 2 black holes

... 4 ottobre 2010 → 2 eyes to see
a new world

FROM ITALY

Italy

"That's what hate looks like . . . that ugly hole."

Please share your thoughts with us:
Share your September 11th story. How have you been changed by the events of September 11th, or what action can you take in the spirit of Tribute to help or educate another?

As I stood looking at the gaping hole left by the tragic events of 911 I thought to myself that's what hate looks like. It look Just like that ugly hole. Hate benefits no one. We should All learn a lesson from this tragedy. Hate hurts the one who hates and the one that the hate is directed At. Teach your children not to hate. Hate destroys as it destroyed the lives of the people lost in the World Trade Center. Love your neighbor As yourself

Virginia

"Thank you God for sparing my husband."

Please share your thoughts with us:
Share your September 11th story. How have you been changed by the events of September 11th, or what action can you take in the spirit of Tribute to help or educate another?

When I think of Sept 11th I think of walking in my home after leaving my children at the bus stop & looking at the T.V. The first plane just hit, I watched the 2nd plane hit. Call my husband (a NYC Firefighter) and He said He's turning around & going in to help — He was on his way home from a night tour. For the next 2 mths I barely saw him & when I did he was exhausted & mentally drained. 9 yrs later, it still is a strong part of our lives. Re-living the day & thinking about all his fallen brothers & our childrens friends who have no Dad now. May the world never forget. Thank You God for sparing my husband

New York

Please share your thoughts with us:

Share your September 11th story. How have you been changed by the events of September 11th, or what action can you take in the spirit of Tribute to help or educate another?

US-MN

have heart
have hope

Never forget
Ne jamais oublie
Nie vegessen
Nunca se olvida
Nikada zaboraviti
Non dimenticare mai
Nu uita
Aldrig glömma

Minnesota

TRANSLATION

Why do terrible things like this happen? Sometimes I wish that this could be a dream. When I see all these pictures, I feel there may be no God. I pray for peace for all the departed souls.

Please share your thoughts with us:
Share your September 11th story. How have you been changed by the events of September 11th, or what action can you take in the spirit of Tribute to help or educate another?

என் இந்த மாதிரியான ஒரு கொடூரம்
நடக்க வேண்டும் சில சமயம் நான்
நினைக்கிறேன். இந்த சமயம் ஒரு கனவாக
இருக்க வேண்டும் என்று. இந்த படங்கள்
எல்லாம் பார்க்கும் போது கடவுள் எது
இருவன் இல்லோ என்று நினைக்க தோன்றுகிறது.
எல்லோருடைய ஆன்மாவும் சாந்தியடைய
வேண்டும் வெங்கிறேன்

Massachusetts

"Still do the right thing despite the personal risk."

Please share your thoughts with us:
Share your September 11ᵗʰ story. How have you been changed
by the events of September 11ᵗʰ, or what action can you take
in the spirit of Tribute to help or educate another?

Its like when Kennedy was shot - everybody knows
what they were doing when the towers came down   I was at
home in a small town in Scotland called Prestwick - I
was ironing ! I just watched this horror on TV and
wept - and kept on weeping In the long term though it
made me so proud that people in extreme conditions still
do the right thing despite the personal risk My heart still
goes out to those who lost loved ones . 9/11 was the
day everything changed

Scotland

TRANSLATION

We were living minute by minute what was taking place in NY, but we could not believe it. It was something impossible to imagine, but something horrible was happening. What desperation, but we saw it all on TV. Now being here on 8/25/08, our feelings are of emptiness, impotence, and of recognition to all those who did the impossible to help.

Please share your thoughts with us:

Share your September 11th story. How have you been changed by the events of September 11th, or what action can you take in the spirit of Tribute to help or educate another?

Vivimos el minuto a minuto de lo que ocurría en NY por la televisión pero no lo podíamos creer Era algo imposible de imaginar, pero estaba pasando Un horror! Que desesperación pero todo lo veíamos por tv Ahora 25/8/08 al estar aca, los sentimientos son de vacío, de impotencia y de reconocimiento a todos los que hicieron lo imposible por ayudar

Montevideo, Uruguay 25/08/08

Uruguay

"I saw long lines of people walking north on Third Avenue."

Please share your thoughts with us:
Share your September 11th story. How have you been changed by the events of September 11th, or what action can you take in the spirit of Tribute to help or educate another?

I LIVED ON THE 14th FLOOR OF AN APARTMENT House on the upper EAST SIDE AND I SAW THE PLANES HIT on TV. I FACED SOUTH AND SAW THE Smoke RISING FROM THE WTC. THEN, AS I CONTINUED TO WATCH I SAW LONG LINES OF PEOPLE WALKING NORTH ON THIRD AVENUE. IT WAS A MASS MIGRATION AND WENT ON FOR HOURS. THESE WERE THE SURVIVORS

Florida

"That's your Grandma's plane."

Please share your thoughts with us:
Share your September 11th story. How have you been changed by the events of September 11th, or what action can you take in the spirit of Tribute to help or educate another?

On September 11th el was woken up to the shock of my life. My Grandma lived in Boston, Ma. and was on her way to California that day for her yearly visit. My mom woke me up and frantically pulled me out to the living room and stared at the tv. ...She then pointed at the screen and said "That's your Grandma's plane." Flight 11, Sept. 11th

California

"With all my heart I wish they were alive."

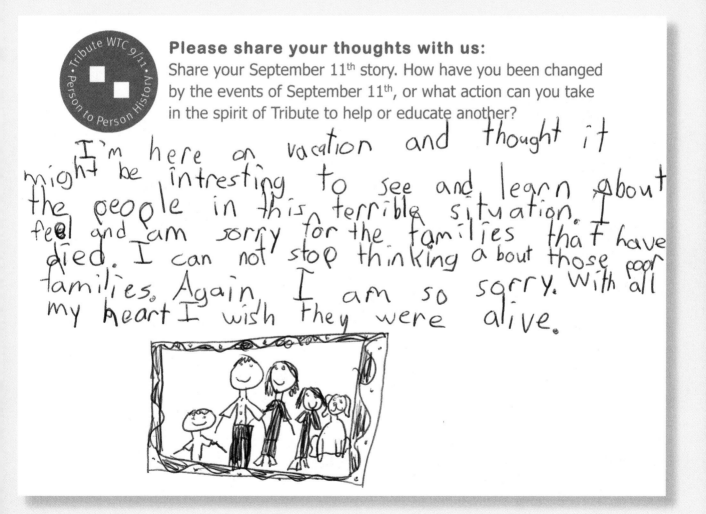

Please share your thoughts with us:
Share your September 11th story. How have you been changed by the events of September 11th, or what action can you take in the spirit of Tribute to help or educate another?

Tribute WTC 9/11 · Person to Person History

I'm here on vacation and thought it might be intresting to see and learn about the people in this terrible situation. I feel and am sorry for the families that have died. I can not stop thinking about those poor families. Again, I am so sorry. With all my heart I wish they were alive.

Kentucky

"Steel is not the greatest metal in the world—the human spirit is."

Please share your thoughts with us:
Share your September 11th story. How have you been changed by the events of September 11th, or what action can you take in the spirit of Tribute to help or educate another?

FDNY

NYPD

NYC

WTC

LOVE

I CAME HOME TO WATCH MY HISTORY CHANGE FOREVER - I WAS 11, AND AM 18 NOW.

THE WORLD IS A VERY DIFFERENT PLACE, WHERE STEEL CAN BE BENT AND TWISTED. BUT MAYBE THAT IS THE POINT - THAT STEEL IS NOT THE GREATEST METAL IN THE WORLD - THE HUMAN SPIRIT IS,

AND THERE IS NOWHERE WHERE THAT SPIRIT IS MORE VIBRANT THAN NEW YORK.

Illinois

Tribute WTC 9/11 · Person to Person History

Please share your thoughts with us:
Share your September 11th story. How have you been changed by the events of September 11th, or what action can you take in the spirit of Tribute to help or educate another?

PEACE!!!

AROUND THE WORLD

2010 – ALWAYS

California

> "So many millions of people . . . restarted the world's heart."

Please share your thoughts with us:
Share your September 11th story. How have you been changed by the events of September 11th, or what action can you take in the spirit of Tribute to help or educate another?

From the disruptive subway ride I was not prepared for the enormity of the World Trade center site, nor the solemnity of so many people — workers, neighbors and visitors, as I tried to find some immediate emotional and visible balance.

Now, almost eight years later, I feel less anger perhaps, but more respect for how so many millions of people from New York, New Jersey, Pennsylvania and the Washington, D.C., that were so tragically and deeply affected, restarted the world's heart — stopped by the unthinkable terror of 9-11. Thank you for your resolve, grace and compassion.

Bend, OR May 20, 2009

Oregon

HOME OF THE BRAVE

"We should honor them in all the ways we can."

Please share your thoughts with us:
Share your September 11th story. How have you been changed by the events of September 11th, or what action can you take in the spirit of Tribute to help or educate another?

I think we should problably help others in many ways alot of people died so I think we should honor them in all the ways we can.

Florida

"The twin towers symbolized the hope of world peace."

Please share your thoughts with us: 11/10/08

Share your September 11th story. How have you been changed by the events of September 11th, or what action can you take in the spirit of Tribute to help or educate another?

I was in fifth grade when the terrorist attacks were made, and viewing this memorium helps me gather a better understanding of ▓ how truly important September 11, 2001 is in American history. The twin towers symbolized the hope of world peace, and their memory still reminds us that we have come a long way, but the journey still has not been completed. It is up to us to change our world.

(Cullman, AL)

Alabama

"We pray not only for the dead but especially for the people who survived."

Please share your thoughts with us:
Share your September 11th story. How have you been changed by the events of September 11th, or what action can you take in the spirit of Tribute to help or educate another?

2008-12-31

There are no words expressing our thoughts about the incident in 2001. What happened is just incredibly sad and we pray not only for the dead but especially for the people who survived and must live with horrible memories... We hope that everybody visiting this exhibition can reflect and re-think as we did and bring peace to another human being.

9/11 will never be forgotten and what was very impressing is that not only one country was shocked, but the whole world.

PEACE, not war!!

Austria

Please share your thoughts with us:
Share your September 11th story. How have you been changed
by the events of September 11th, or what action can you take
in the spirit of Tribute to help or educate another?

I wasn't ready to say
goodbye like
that.

California

We must learn to love one another and know that these types of events should never repeat themselves, because otherwise we would be ending ourselves. This sorrow should never be repeated.

Please share your thoughts with us:
Share your September 11th story. How have you been changed by the events of September 11th, or what action can you take in the spirit of Tribute to help or educate another?

TENEMOS QUE APRENDER A AMARNOS

Y SABER QUE ESTOS EVENTOS NO

VUELVAN A REPETIRSE NUNCA, PORQUE

ESTARIAMOS ARABANDO CON NOSOTROS MISMOS

ESTE DOLOR NUNCA MAS DEBE REPETIRSE

Mexico

Please share your thoughts with us:
Share your September 11th story. How have you been changed by the events of September 11th, or what action can you take in the spirit of Tribute to help or educate another?

NEVER AGAIN — NOT IN ANY

COUNTRY!

U.K.

United Kingdom

Please share your thoughts with us:
Share your September 11th story. How have you been changed by the events of September 11th, or what action can you take in the spirit of Tribute to help or educate another?

EL MEJOR HOMENAJE A LAS VÍCTIMAS DEL 11·S, A LAS VÍCTIMAS DE TODO TIPO DE TERRORISMO, ES MANTENER EL TESTIMONIO DE UN FUTURO SIN MIEDO, SIN TEMOR AL OTRO. ESE DEBE SER EL LEGADO PARA NUESTROS HIJOS Y LAS GENERACIONES VENIDERAS.
THE PAIN DONT WIN, NEVER.
(CON ADRIÁN EN EL PENSAMIENTO)

Spain

> "There are many many more good/kind acts to every bad/evil one."

Please share your thoughts with us:
Share your September 11th story. How have you been changed by the events of September 11th, or what action can you take in the spirit of Tribute to help or educate another?

To the world,

I am a muslim, and a true muslim loves everyone, no matter what colour, creed or background. The so called muslims who attacked the towers on September 11th were **not** true muslims. You have to feel sorry for these people and what was so bad + evil in their heads that they decided to carry out such henerdous acts on their fellow-humans. Only by loving thy neighbour can we begin to make this world a better place. There are many many more good/kind acts to every bad/evil one.
Remember that ~ love

uk

United Kingdom

Please share your thoughts with us:
Share your September 11th story. How have you been changed by the events of September 11th, or what action can you take in the spirit of Tribute to help or educate another?

WHY can't we just
won't we just
is it so hard to just

LOVE

Michigan

TRANSLATION

We have wept and have grieved and lost hope, but from today may the way we treat one another be loving regardless of from where we hail.

Please share your thoughts with us:
Share your September 11th story. How have you been changed by the events of September 11th, or what action can you take in the spirit of Tribute to help or educate another?

na 'emaung ang ten na masudramanga iten

ulja ten a kemasi tucu a namakaljivaljivak

ini ka pusenemanu caucawan

ulja izua ta pazeka tua timaimanga

ti dremedreman

96 8/5

Taiwan

"What used to be the icon of New York."

Please share your thoughts with us:
Share your September 11th story. How have you been changed
by the events of September 11th, or what action can you take
in the spirit of Tribute to help or educate another?

Not an American, not a New Yorker, not even from
this continent, but the sadness that engulfed everyone's
hearts resides in mine as I walked around ground zero,
thinking how it was like on 9/11, empathizing with the victims.
All across the world, we share the same humanity and
common understanding of love. As much as Americans will
never forget, so will I not forget my walk around what
used to be the icon of New York.

— Singapore —

Singapore

"I'm glad to see the volunteer spirit here."

Please share your thoughts with us:
Share your September 11th story. How have you been changed by the events of September 11th, or what action can you take in the spirit of Tribute to help or educate another?

We can't ~~see~~ meet victims again and they never come back here, however we ~~could~~ are still alive and we can hope world peace As long as I live, I hope the world where is no tragedy And I'm glad to see the volunteer spirit here. Now, my country, Japan, ~~xxxxxxx~~ faces a serious crisis. A lot of people were dead by big earthquake and tsunami We Japanese have to get over this crisis like New Yorkers I want to help Japanese who is injured like New Yorkers who helped casualties in 11th of September I'm sorry for my poor English It's very good for me to visit here today Thanks a lot.

Japan

"We share the same humanity."

Please share your thoughts with us:
Share your September 11th story. How have you been changed
by the events of September 11th, or what action can you take
in the spirit of Tribute to help or educate another?

May 25, 2009

I live so far away – another country,
another continent, another culture.
But we share the same humanity,
and as I shed tears then in another
country, another continent, I shed
tears now that finally I am here,
in your country reliving, sharing your
pain and your loss. God bless America!

Philippines

TRANSLATION

We express our great sorrow to all the men, women, and children who lost their lives during the calamity. We the people of Papua New Guinea stand with you to defend against terror in this part of the world. God bless America.

Please share your thoughts with us:

Share your September 11th story. How have you been changed by the events of September 11th, or what action can you take in the spirit of Tribute to help or educate another?

Bikpela toksori i go long ol mam/meri na pikinini i lusim laip long dispela birua. ~~belong~~ Mipela ol pipol belong Papua New Guinea i sanap wantaim you long pasim rot belong tera insait long dispela hap bilong world. God i ken blessim America.

Papua New Guinea

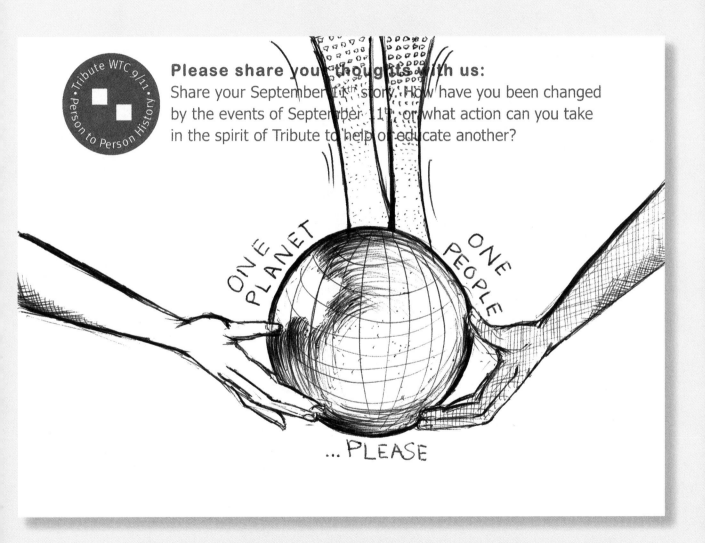

Please share your thoughts with us:
Share your September 11th story. How have you been changed
by the events of September 11th, or what action can you take
in the spirit of Tribute to help or educate another?

ONE PLANET

ONE PEOPLE

... PLEASE

California

Please share your thoughts with us:
Share your September 11th story. How have you been changed
by the events of September 11th, or what action can you take
in the spirit of Tribute to help or educate another?

This reminds me that
the world is
one village,
one family.

Australia

Australia

"A growing responsibility and awareness as a global citizen."

Please share your thoughts with us:
Share your September 11th story. How have you been changed by the events of September 11th, or what action can you take in the spirit of Tribute to help or educate another?

I was a junior at Cresskill High School on 9-11-01 and I remember the day vividly. Fear, uncertainty, and general restlessness and panic flowed into every crevice within each student's mind. I have since that day embraced a growing responsibility and awareness as a global citizen – not just as an American – in collaborating with neighboring nations and their people in overcoming differences that oftentimes separate us.

New York

TRANSLATION

This day became a point of reflection in the lives of all human beings, no matter what sex, race, religion, nationality, or political belief. We all have negative feelings towards those that committed this massacre, so we should continue with the unity this brought, the hugs, the support among strangers, the humanitarian work, the tears of support for someone else's pain. Let's learn the lesson of unity and peace. Let us become one family.

Please share your thoughts with us:
Share your September 11th story. How have you been changed by the events of September 11th, or what action can you take in the spirit of Tribute to help or educate another?

Este día supuso un punto de inflexión en las vidas de todo ser humano, sin importar sexo, raza, religión, nacionalidad, ideal político. Todos tenemos sentimientos negativos hacia los que cometieron esta amasacre, entonces.. por qué no quedarnos con la unión que supuso, los abrazos y consuelo entre descocado, con las labores humanitarias, con las lágrimas de desconsuelo por el sufrimiento ajeno, APRENDAMOS LA LECCIÓN de la unión y la PAZ, seamos una única familia
— SPAIN-

Spain

"What happened on September 11 shakes every inch of me."

Please share your thoughts with us:
Share your September 11th story. How have you been changed by the events of September 11th, or what action can you take in the spirit of Tribute to help or educate another?

I cant believe I finally made it here. I'm nervous & there is a weird feeling in me even today after so many years. I'am an Indian origin, who grew in a Muslim-oriented Middle eastern country of Qatar & now settled in Australia. Having witnessed so many cultures myself, its hard for me to think there can be differences in humans in name of race & religion. What happened on sept 11 shakes every inch of me even today. What assurity do I have for a well rounded safe future for my kids if I have them? Such hatredness, such anger, such fanatism & fundamentalism will only cause more n more harm. Today as I sit here n write, my heart goes out to those families who lost their loved ones, those incredible fire fighters, those volunteers who came forward. GOD BLESS THEM! WE WILL SURELY NEVER FORGET!

Australia

"This event brought out the best in people."

Please share your thoughts with us:
Share your September 11th story. How have you been changed by the events of September 11th, or what action can you take in the spirit of Tribute to help or educate another?

This exhibition has brought me to thinking that the people who committed these cruel acts have failed in their attempt to create anger and hatred. All around me I can see people who have given everything to help others, to show love and compassion for others. This event brought out the best in people. I believe that there is a lot of good in humanity. We should use this experience to help bring the world together. I wish for peace in the hearts of those who lost loved ones.

ENGLAND

United Kingdom

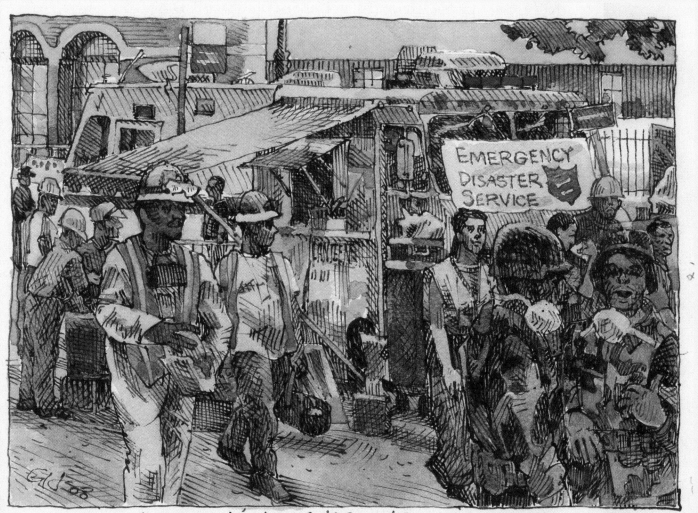

Greenwich Street - 9-'01

"My heart is shattered for the families left behind."

Please share your thoughts with us:
Share your September 11th story. How have you been changed
by the events of September 11th, or what action can you take
in the spirit of Tribute to help or educate another?

I don't think words or phrases will
ever describe this trauma,
My heart is shattered for the families
left behind
& my sincerest heartfelt love & honour
go to all those heroes who tried to piece
it together
Although from London—God Bless America,
My love for this place is eternal

United Kingdom

"Made me change my whole perspective on what's important in life."

Please share your thoughts with us:
Share your September 11th story. How have you been changed
by the events of September 11th, or what action can you take
in the spirit of Tribute to help or educate another?

Sept 11 made me change my
whole perspective on whats important
in life – I left my wall street
job and moved to DC to work for a
nonprofit – teen helping young people to
be empowered by service –
this is so important any young people
need to better understand for the day changed
lives forever – everywhere –

Washington, D.C.

"Peace starts from within."

Please share your thoughts with us:
Share your September 11th story. How have you been changed by the events of September 11th, or what action can you take in the spirit of Tribute to help or educate another?

Thank you for this Wonderful Memorial,
Peace starts from within — It is my hope
that we teach our children about personal
peace, community peace & global peace.
It is my hope that this becomes a priority in
school curriculums.   ♡

Australia   25/6/10

Australia

Please share your thoughts with us:

Share your September 11th story. How have you been changed by the events of September 11th, or what action can you take in the spirit of Tribute to help or educate another?

TO REBUILD WE NEED A WORLD OF PEACE

07 August 09

ITALY

Italy

"To live a more productive, meaningful & loving life."

Please share your thoughts with us:
Share your September 11th story. How have you been changed by the events of September 11th, or what action can you take in the spirit of Tribute to help or educate another?

To those souls with whom I used to walk the corridors of the WTC, I'm inspired by your lives to live a more productive, meaningful & loving life.

We miss you, we love you!

France

"All I know is that this site shows the strength of the human spirit."

Please share your thoughts with us:
Share your September 11th story. How have you been changed
by the events of September 11th, or what action can you take
in the spirit of Tribute to help or educate another?

Just like everyone I knew, I remember 9/11
as if it were yesterday. In a total state of
shock, we gazed at the television all day
long, but couldn't comprehend what we saw.
And now that we are here, I still cannot
fully grasp it. All I know is that this site
shows the strength of the human spirit, and
it teaches us to love and respect one-another
and to take care of eachother – no matter
what country, background or religion we're from.

The Netherlands

"It's the news—not a movie."

Please share your thoughts with us:
Share your September 11th story. How have you been changed by the events of September 11th, or what action can you take in the spirit of Tribute to help or educate another?

My Grandfather was having a very complicated surgery that morning. My brother & I awoke at 5:30 AM with our grandmother to be by our grandfather's side. I walked into the kitchen, where my grandmother was watching TV. I said "Grandma that's a pretty violent movie to be watching at this hour!" Her ~~face~~ faced was pale white and she said "This is really happening - it's the news - not a movie." We all watched in horror as the second plane struck. My Grandfather survived that day - but we will forever mourn those didn't. God Bless.

Canada

"I use 9/11 as a memory . . . and what could have been."

Please share your thoughts with us:
Share your September 11th story. How have you been changed
by the events of September 11th, or what action can you take
in the spirit of Tribute to help or educate another?

As the granddaughter of a victim I
use 9/11 as a memory as what was and
what could have been. The entire US was
impacted - the entire world - remembering
to fight fear + hatred w/ love + strength is
challenging but emperative to teach our children.

Anonymous

"Today I kneel before them and pray."

Please share your thoughts with us:
Share your September 11th story. How have you been changed by the events of September 11th, or what action can you take in the spirit of Tribute to help or educate another?

Last time I was in New York I stood on top of those amazing towers. Today I kneel before them and pray.

United Kingdom

Please share your thoughts with us:
Share your September 11th story. How have you been changed
by the events of September 11th, or what action can you take
in the spirit of Tribute to help or educate another?

GOD BLESS YOU

1/30/11
Buenos Aires
Argentina

Argentina

"But the spirit of love from everyone was tremendous to see."

Please share your thoughts with us:
Share your September 11th story. How have you been changed by the events of September 11th, or what action can you take in the spirit of Tribute to help or educate another?

I was in my newsroom near Toronto and had just finished a newscast on the radio when I looked up at the newswire to see a plane had hit WTC. I immediately turned to CNN and saw the second plane hit the tower. The wire services went crazy for that first 15-30 minutes. I scrambled to get the words together and myself together to tell our radio stations listeners what was happening. It was the hardest thing I'd ever done as a newsbroadcaster that was 8 years ago. That day our newsroom rallied together to put together a fundraiser for our community, the Niagara Region a border town with our friends to the south in NY to raise money to the families and Som. We raised over 50,000 dollars. It was all we could do to ease their own sorrow for what happened that day. But the spirit of love from everyone was tremendous to see. I can say years later being here for the first time, the memory of a terrible time is as fresh as ever and will Never be forgotten! Toronto, Canada

Canada

"Such an outstandingly positive response."

Please share your thoughts with us:
Share your September 11th story. How have you been changed by the events of September 11th, or what action can you take in the spirit of Tribute to help or educate another?

I was reminded of the true spirit of humanity that flowed forth in all of the outpouring of grief and help from people all over the U.S. and the world. It is hard to continue to be cynical in the face of such an outstandingly positive response by millions of people to their act of terrorism.

Anonymous

"Man is great to think and build so beautiful things."

Please share your thoughts with us:
Share your September 11th story. How have you been changed
by the events of September 11th, or what action can you take
in the spirit of Tribute to help or educate another?

Salii sulla Torre nel 1991 e lì pensai quanto
l'uomo fosse grande nell'avere pensato e
costruito una simile bellezza.
Mai avrei pensato, fosse anche capace di
simile distruzione.

I went up the Tower in 1991 and there I thought
how the man is great to think and build so
beautiful things
Never I should have thought be able to destroy too

Italy

Please share your thoughts with us:
Share your September 11th story. How have you been changed
by the events of September 11th, or what action can you take
in the spirit of Tribute to help or educate another?

ITALY

Italy

"This pain, is not only America's pain but that of the world."

Please share your thoughts with us:
Share your September 11th story. How have you been changed
by the events of September 11th, or what action can you take
in the spirit of Tribute to help or educate another?

I brought my group of high school international
exchange students here to see, feel and understand
what 9-11 means to America, what 9-11 means
to the world This pain, is not only America's pain
but that of the world and the children of the
world need to understand so that not only
is this not forgotten but prevented in the future

iE-USA

Florida

Please share your thoughts with us:
Share your September 11th story. How have you been changed by the events of September 11th, or what action can you take in the spirit of Tribute to help or educate another?

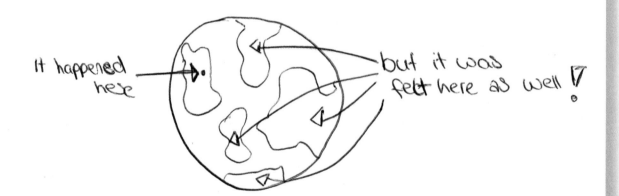

It happened here — but it was felt here as well!

Germany

Germany

"This was America's worst and best hour."

Please share your thoughts with us:
Share your September 11th story. How have you been changed by the events of September 11th, or what action can you take in the spirit of Tribute to help or educate another?

I WAS ON HOLIDAY IN FRANCE ON SEPTEMBER 11TH. THE VERY NEXT DAY, I WAS IN A SUPERMARKET IN THE MIDDLE OF THE COUNTRYSIDE, AND AT 12 NOON, A VOICE CAME OVER THE TANNOY TO ASK FOR TWO MINUTES OF SILENCE IN RESPECT FOR THE VICTIMS. EVERYONE, ABSOLUTELY EVERYONE, STAYED ABSOLUTELY SILENT. THE NEWSPAPER HEADLINE SAID "NOUS SOMMES TOUS AMERICAINS" - "WE ARE ALL AMERICANS". WE WERE, AND ARE, ALL AMERICANS, AND CONTINUE TO STAND SHOULDER TO SHOULDER WITH OUR AMERICAN FRIENDS. THIS WAS AMERICA'S WORST AND BEST HOUR, FOR OUT OF THE INCOMPREHENSION OF THOSE EVENTS HAS COME THE LOVE AND RECONSTRUCTION THAT THIS CENTRE EXEMPLIFIES.

United Kingdom

Please share your thoughts with us:
Share your September 11th story. How have you been changed
by the events of September 11th, or what action can you take
in the spirit of Tribute to help or educate another?

THANKs TO ALL WHO HELPED
LIFT OUR SPIRITS AFTER 9/11

FDNY

New York

131

"Celebrate life and be grateful for everything we have!"

Please share your thoughts with us:
Share your September 11th story. How have you been changed by the events of September 11th, or what action can you take in the spirit of Tribute to help or educate another?

May this tragedy teach us to promote peace & understanding by seeing a fellow-human being in every person we meet, and to celebrate life and be grateful for everything we have !

Italy

Italy

"I am inspired to start here in my heart."

Please share your thoughts with us:
Share your September 11th story. How have you been changed by the events of September 11th, or what action can you take in the spirit of Tribute to help or educate another?

This pain all around me brings me to tears. Why do people hate so much? People inflict pain on others to make their point, to get their own way, to exalt themselves over others, to say "I am better than you!"
This happens in our hearts every day on every level — in our marriages and families, as we drive on the highway, as we wait in lines, in our neighborhoods and communities across the world. There is divorce, cursing tongues and shaking fists and pointing fingers and angry looks. I am inspired to start here in my heart. We all need to say "NO!" to the hatred that resides in us all.

California

"We build our new towers in a new world."

An age ago, the messages on these walls might have been about Victory, triumph, vengence or strength. Now they are about a moral strength: love, condolence, learning and longing for peace. That is a reflection of what the world is coming to value as it grows wiser. We build our new towers in a new world, and it will continue to become a better world, as long as we never give up, give in or give way to hating. God bless this country and its people.

United States

134

Please share your thoughts with us:
Share your September 11th story. How have you been changed by the events of September 11th, or what action can you take in the spirit of Tribute to help or educate another?

Tribute WTC 9/11 · Person to Person History

27-07-'09

To a new Skyline

Holland

The Netherlands

"Every moment has become more precious to me."

Please share your thoughts with us:

Share your September 11th story. How have you been changed by the events of September 11th, or what action can you take in the spirit of Tribute to help or educate another?

07/16/09

My father was lucky enough to escape death on 9/11, at the pentagon, and because of this every moment has become more precious to me. Little arguments, trivialities all disappear in the wake of the memories that come crashing down upon remembring how fragile life is and how quickly that which we love can disappear.

It would be so easy to forget the message of 9/11 as tragedy is often hard to ponder, yet we MUST not forget.

The World would be better if everyone learned to love.

United States

Please share your thoughts with us:
Share your September 11th story. How have you been changed
by the events of September 11th, or what action can you take
in the spirit of Tribute to help or educate another?

Everyone has a story!

NEVER stop listening

South Africa

"Time cannot erase the memory of your face."

Please share your thoughts with us:
Share your September 11th story. How have you been changed by the events of September 11th, or what action can you take in the spirit of Tribute to help or educate another?

Remembering Andrew

Time Can not erase
the memory of your face
It hold a Special Place
Such beauty and Grace
You were Stolen from this place
Gone without a trace
Your compassion and Devotion
Can never be replaced
Time Can not erase this feeling
I must face
without your sweet embrace the
Earth's a different place
Time can not erase the Courage
on your face as you
Climbed the burning towers
to Save the human face
Yet time can not erase
I long to See your face.
L-132
FDNY

New York

138

"From that moment on the entire day moved so slowly."

Please share your thoughts with us:
Share your September 11th story. How have you been changed by the events of September 11th, or what action can you take in the spirit of Tribute to help or educate another?

I was at my boarding academy when the office secretary yelled out. From that moment on the entire day moved so slowly. We all gathered in the apt. of the girls dean, as many prayed for the safety of their loved ones. I held a good friend as he cried realizing both of his parents had perished. My life will never be the same

Missouri

Please share your thoughts with us:
Share your September 11th story. How have you been changed by the events of September 11th, or what action can you take in the spirit of Tribute to help or educate another?

Anonymous

"On loud speaker phone with New York when the first plane hit."

Please share your thoughts with us:
Share your September 11th story. How have you been changed by the events of September 11th, or what action can you take in the spirit of Tribute to help or educate another?

I WORKED FOR THE BANK OF NEW YORK IN LONDON. ON 9/11 AT 1.58PM WE WERE ON LOUD SPEAKER PHONE WITH NEW YORK WHEN THE FIRST PLANE HIT. WE LOST 3 PEOPLE THAT DAY.

United Kingdom

"On September 11th, 2001 all state lines became erased."

On September 11th, 2001 all state lines became erased. I became a New Yorker, even beyond that I became an American. The World became a bigger place, but in some since it became smaller. You were my brothers & sisters. and I grieved with You over our loss.

Georgia

Please share your thoughts with us:

Share your September 11th story. How have you been changed by the events of September 11th, or what action can you take in the spirit of Tribute to help or educate another?

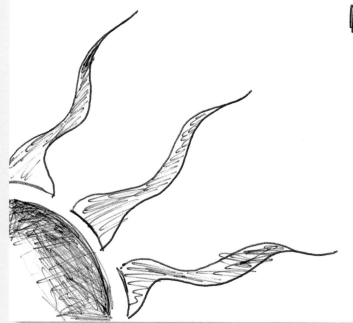

Αιωνια

η γτηγη

ΑΓΑΠΗ ΚΑΙ ΕΙΡΗΝΗ

ΣΕ ΟΛΟ ΤΟΝ ΚΟΣΜΟ

ΚΥΠΡΟΣ

Cyprus

"I wondered had we learned anything at all?"

Please share your thoughts with us:
Share your September 11th story. How have you been changed
by the events of September 11th, or what action can you take
in the spirit of Tribute to help or educate another?

I was at home in the UK when I watched
what happened and I knew the world would never
be the same. The Feb after I visited the USA +
NYC and stood + hugged a man who would have
celebrated his 25th wedding anniversary if his wife
had survived 9/11. Some years later I lost a
close friend in the London bombings and I
wondered had we learned anything at all?

United Kingdom

144

"Running in Central Park, that saved my life!"

Please share your thoughts with us:
Share your September 11th story. How have you been changed
by the events of September 11th, or what action can you take
in the spirit of Tribute to help or educate another?

I was on my way to the
WTC this morning of 11th Sept
2001 for Breakfast on the
windows on the world Restaurant
But I was late due to running
in central park, that saved
my Life! And today I am here
with my wife to celebrate our
marriage Day. But also to remember
this Day that changed the world
and our lifes. Thanks for beeing
here!

Belgium

"I was astonished by what followed—by the solidarity of people."

Please share your thoughts with us:
Share your September 11th story. How have you been changed
by the events of September 11th, or what action can you take
in the spirit of Tribute to help or educate another?

I was necessarily shocked by 9-11 events but
I was astonished by what followed – by the
solidarity of people, by determination
of those who had worked on Ground Zero
for 9 months. Thus the terrible event in
the end reignited in my sceptical
European soul new confidence in people
+ in their ability to withstand the hard
trials.
                                        Prague

Czech Republic

"My students wanted to do something for the nation after 9/11."

Please share your thoughts with us:
Share your September 11th story. How have you been changed
by the events of September 11th, or what action can you take
in the spirit of Tribute to help or educate another?

I teach middle school in North Carolina.
My students wanted to do something for the
nation after 9/11. We started a Dance
Marathon. It is still going in 2008. Three
middle schools have raised $80,000 for Duke
and North Carolina Children's Hospitals.

North Carolina

"To my Brothers on FDNY you are the best of the best, without a doubt."

Please share your thoughts with us:
Share your September 11th story. How have you been changed by the events of September 11th, or what action can you take in the spirit of Tribute to help or educate another?

I was here in late October 2001, and as a Fire Fighter from Canada, I Felt for my 343 Brothers that didn't make it home that day that were "on the job" it is my duty to help in the recovery of people so citizens and emergency workers who perished that day that closure would come to their families. To my Brothers on FDNY you are the best of the best, without a doubt. I hope that all FDNY members "Play Safe "everyday "on the job". God Bless Vaughan F.D.

Canada

Please share your thoughts with us:
Share your September 11th story. How have you been changed
by the events of September 11th, or what action can you take
in the spirit of Tribute to help or educate another?

Italy

149

"A complete stranger came up to me and hugged & held me."

Please share your thoughts with us:
Share your September 11th story. How have you been changed
by the events of September 11th, or what action can you take
in the spirit of Tribute to help or educate another?

On that Day I was in my Highschool classroom + a girl ran in saying she had seen a plane crash into the twin towers from her ride on the ferry. I felt so sad, scared, empty, distanced + unattached that whole day. When I got home and saw it on the news, I cried. New Yorkers banded together. We empathized, loved, cherished, helped, and honored each other. Just now, as I stood shaking + crying upstairs in the gallery, a complete stranger came up to me and hugged + held me. We cried together. Not knowing anything of each other except the humanity + love from surviving 9/11.

New York

"The whole day, the locals helped us."

Please share your thoughts with us:
Share your September 11th story. How have you been changed by the events of September 11th, or what action can you take in the spirit of Tribute to help or educate another?

I was living abroad *in Honduras* as a teacher that year, and one morning my assistant ran into the class and told me that I had to go. I walked out into the yard and found a community combi van waiting for me and the other teachers who were wandering out one at a time. It was in the van that they told us about the Twin Towers. The whole day, the locals helped us, brought food, placed phone calls, and it was there that I experienced the world's care for our tragedy.

United States

"Every time I think of that day . . . my heart breaks a little."

Please share your thoughts with us:
Share your September 11th story. How have you been changed by the events of September 11th, or what action can you take in the spirit of Tribute to help or educate another?

I was in the 8th grade when it happened and it was the first and only time I saw my father cry. Seven years have passed and every time I think of that day, the families that lost their loved ones, and the ones that risked their lives, my heart breaks a little

Florida

"My family & I are very blessed to have each other."

Please share your thoughts with us:
Share your September 11th story. How have you been changed
by the events of September 11th, or what action can you take
in the spirit of Tribute to help or educate another?

To show love, kindness & Compassion
to those that are in need
My family & I are very blessed
to have each other.
We miss Todd very much

United States

"You who have contributed can rest."

Please share your thoughts with us:
Share your September 11th story. How have you been changed by the events of September 11th, or what action can you take in the spirit of Tribute to help or educate another?

8 years later.

i am 23 y.o. now. finally able to comprehend all of this. i am sorry. sorry that i was young and naive when this happened. i was unable to offer anything.

but.

i promise. my generation and i. as we come of age. wiser. and with this chip on my shoulder. our shoulders. to continue the proud cultural tradition of American perseverance and achievement.

i am a Filipino-American. i promise to do all i can now. so that you who have contributed can rest. i know i am young. i know i am no saint. but allow me. allow the next generation. to do our part.

United States

Chambers Street, 9·'01

"I will never forget. I feel like I have finally come full circle."

Please share your thoughts with us:
Share your September 11th story. How have you been changed by the events of September 11th, or what action can you take in the spirit of Tribute to help or educate another?

Sept. 11, 2001 · I was serving in the Army stationed in Germany. We were in our final formation of the day when the news broke. From that day on the security posture of the military changed. Eight years later and one tour in Iraq this is my first visit to the WTC site. It is easy to become desensitized by all that I have seen and experienced while serving. The memorial has brought me back to day one (Sept 11). My heart is broken for the many families touched by this tragedy I will never forget. I feel like I have finally come full circle.
God Bless America.
us Army

Texas

"Which religion on this earth teaches us to kill humans?"

Please share your thoughts with us:
Share your September 11th story. How have you been changed by the events of September 11th, or what action can you take in the spirit of Tribute to help or educate another?

I am from India. A Sikh woman
I just want to ask which Religion
on this earth Teaches us to
kill human??? Our fellow!??
Any ANSWER?????

Jan 16th 2010

India

"I realised . . . the power of human resilience."

Please share your thoughts with us:
Share your September 11th story. How have you been changed
by the events of September 11th, or what action can you take
in the spirit of Tribute to help or educate another?

9/11 has always to me been a
remote disaster.

Visiting this site today a realised
the enormity of this crime and the
depth of human cruelty.
But also the power of human resilience.
God bless the victims

KENYA
OCTOBER 13, 2008

Kenya

"I remember how beautiful the sky was."

Please share your thoughts with us:
Share your September 11th story. How have you been changed
by the events of September 11th, or what action can you take
in the spirit of Tribute to help or educate another?

On Sept 11, 2001 I was ~~was~~ with my
entire family, & everyone who loved us most
burying my father. And I remember how
beautiful the sky was and a day of peace
for my dad who had been so sick for so
long. I remember how we first heard about
the planes. And how flight 93 flew over
us at the cemetery in Ohio, we could
see how low it was. The picture of
Father Judge reminds me of my 5 Brothers
carring my dads coffin at the exact same time
and ~~Father~~ 2. looked exactly like my dad.

Ohio

TRANSLATION

Seeing the photographs, the movie clips, the personal items, the space . . . you live (feel) the pain, the indignation for all those gone, the orphans, the relatives . . . At the same time, you see the hope because there is humanity and heroism still in the world. On that day I had my 21st birthday and it was the worst in my life. . . . I will never forget the anxiety we had for the friends, the indignation towards terrorism, and the pain of the families. May God rest their souls and give strength and courage to those left behind. . . .

CYPRUS

Please share your thoughts with us:

Share your September 11th story. How have you been changed by the events of September 11th, or what action can you take in the spirit of Tribute to help or educate another?

Βλέποντας το φωτογραφίες, εις ταινίες, τα προσωπικά αντικείμενα το χώρο... ζεις τον πόνο, την αγανάκτηση, των όσων έφυγαν, των ορφανών, των συγγενών...

Ταυτόχρονα βλέπεις την ελπίδα γιατί υπάρχει ΑΝΘΡΩΠΙΑ και ΗΡΩΪΣΜΟΣ ακόμα στον κόσμο.

Εκείνη την μέρα είχα τα 21st γενέθλιά μου και ήταν τα χειρότερα της ζωής μου... Δεν θα ξεχάσω ποτέ την αγωνία που είχαμε για τας φίλας, την αγανάκτηση για την τρομοκρατία, και τον πόνο των οικογενειών.

Ο Θεός ΑΣ ΑΝΑΠΑΥΣΕΙ ΤΗ ΨΥΧΗ ΤΟΥΣ, και ΝΑ ΔΙΝΕΙ ΔΥΝΑΜΗ ΚΑΙ ΚΟΥΡΑΓΙΟ ΣΕ ΑΥΤΟΥΣ ΠΟΥ ΕΜΕΙΝΑΝ...

Cyprus

Please share your thoughts with us:
Share your September 11th story. How have you been changed
by the events of September 11th, or what action can you take
in the spirit of Tribute to help or educate another?

(Argentinian)
1/11/2010

Argentina

"At that time he was only 9 months old."

Please share your thoughts with us:
Share your September 11th story. How have you been changed by the events of September 11th, or what action can you take in the spirit of Tribute to help or educate another?

Heard the news on the radio and remember that I felt it surrealistic and non-human Who would actually do such a thing I also remember how I could tell it to my son At that time he was only 9 months old How can you tell or explain actions as 9/11th You can't Thus it's a releif to me showing him this memorial today almost 10 years after I believe he understood the madness and impact it gave us all recieving the news that day A lot of thougts goes to every victim, relatives and volunteer/workers   with love

Denmark

"I saw my mother shedding tears."

The only times that I saw my mother shedding tears were once my grandmother passed away and the second time was on Sep. 11, 2001.

From Iran

Iran

"I teach my students about the lessons of 9/11."

Please share your thoughts with us:
Share your September 11th story. How have you been changed by the events of September 11th, or what action can you take in the spirit of Tribute to help or educate another?

I remember the event of 9/11 unfolding on TV. Told myself then that I must make the pilgrimage. Today, my first visit to NY, I came here to honour, pray and pay tribute to those who perished. May God bless them. I teach my students about the lessons of 9/11 - of peace, heroism, courage, forgiveness but most important, of LOVE and HUMANITY.

singapore 19 May 08

Singapore

"All the faces I had seen two days prior flashed in my mind."

Please share your thoughts with us:
Share your September 11th story. How have you been changed by the events of September 11th, or what action can you take in the spirit of Tribute to help or educate another?

On September 9, 2001 my family and I came to NYC for vacation That Sunday we visited the Twin Towers and ate lunch on the 109th floor since world of windows was closed We returned home at 2:00 am on Sept 11, 2001 I remember waking up and seeing on the news the towers crumbling to the ground All the faces I had seen two days prior flashed in my mind I immediately began praying for all and crying A day I'll never forget !!

Oklahoma

TRANSLATION

When the disaster of the twin towers occurred, I was in Cuenca, Ecuador, a city that 80% of the Ecuadorian immigrants to the U.S. are from. Pain, worry, and a sense of powerlessness filled all of the corners of my city. Many people whom I love and know lived here, including my best friend who was listed among the disappeared. It took me 3 weeks to learn that she was okay. The collapse of the twin towers was a universal sorrow and although I hadn't been to this country I felt a part of it. Now I am here on vacation and I am taking with me an image of New York without the twin towers.

Please share your thoughts with us:

Share your September 11th story. How have you been changed by the events of September 11th, or what action can you take in the spirit of Tribute to help or educate another?

ECUADOR

Dios bendiga a todas las víctimas y sus familias.

Cuando ocurrió el desastre de las torres gemelas, me encontraba en Cuenca - Ecuador, ciudad de la que pertenecen un 80% de los migrantes ecuatorianos en este país, el dolor, la preocupación y la impotencia llegó a todos los rincones de mi ciudad, mucha gente a la que quiero y conosco vivian acá, incluso mi mejor amiga apareció entre los desaparecidos, me duró 3 semanas para saber que ella estaba OK., la caída de las Torres gemelas fue un dolor universal, aunque no conocía este país me sentía parte de él, ahora vine de vacaciones y me voy con una imagen de New York sin torres gemelas.

Ecuador

Please share your thoughts with us:
Share your September 11th story. How have you been changed
by the events of September 11th, or what action can you take
in the spirit of Tribute to help or educate another?

China

"The idea of not having security finally entered our own world."

Please share your thoughts with us:
Share your September 11th story. How have you been changed by the events of September 11th, or what action can you take in the spirit of Tribute to help or educate another?

September ~~eleventh~~ twelfth Two-thousand One

when everything ~~was~~ in the world stopped
many countries grieving their loses
many families mourning their pain
everyone was making their efforts
but no one feeling closure
the idea of not having security finally
entered our own world

California

"My 3 young daughters asked if they were safe."

Please share your thoughts with us:
Share your September 11ᵗʰ story. How have you been changed
by the events of September 11ᵗʰ, or what action can you take
in the spirit of Tribute to help or educate another?

My 3 young daughters asked
if they were safe I reassured
them living in rural PA was
safe... but they watched the
Flight 93 fly low over their
playground in Ligonier PA It crashed
3 air miles beyond. God Bless all of USA.

Pennsylvania

TRANSLATION

Never again should this take place in the name of whatever the cause may be. No cause can justify the death of innocent people. I hope that this event will be a remembered date in history for all human beings of all nations. Let us make this earth a place of peace and of mutual understanding. We can resolve differences better by more peaceful means, by dialogue, and by respecting each other. God didn't give any man that right to take the life of other men in the name of political causes or ideologies.

Please share your thoughts with us:

Share your September 11th story. How have you been changed by the events of September 11th, or what action can you take in the spirit of Tribute to help or educate another?

Senegal

Please share your thoughts with us:
Share your September 11th story. How have you been changed
by the events of September 11th, or what action can you take
in the spirit of Tribute to help or educate another?

We have only one "a"
It is us who decide where
to put it.

Indonesia

171

"We share the same pain."

Please share your thoughts with us:
Share your September 11th story. How have you been changed by the events of September 11th, or what action can you take in the spirit of Tribute to help or educate another?

Even though I'm an Aussie and I live across the ocean, seeing the devestation caused by the September 11 attacks makes me realise that even though we may compete against each other in everything from finance to sport, we are ONE! We share the same pain.

Australia

"We all should be together to bear such awful grief."

Please share your thoughts with us:
Share your September 11th story. How have you been changed by the events of September 11th, or what action can you take in the spirit of Tribute to help or educate another?

I can't express my feelings right now. This tragedy run through our hearts also. I think in such cases we all should be together to bear such awful grief. Thank you for the saved memories.

photojournalist, kyrgyzstan

R.I.P.

Kyrgyzstan

"My prayers remain with the people of New York."

Please share your thoughts with us:
Share your September 11th story. How have you been changed
by the events of September 11th, or what action can you take
in the spirit of Tribute to help or educate another?

I was in my office in Windhoek, Namibia. It was a
beautiful spring afternoon — when I saw armagedon
on our TV screens. Ever since, the fate of the
"citizens" of the Twin Towers and the bravery of
the firemen has been in my heart. There is not a
day that goes by that I do not silently mourn
for every life lost. My prayers remain with the
people of New York and the United States.
        I will never forget
        ("Ek sal nooit vergeet nie")
        I love New York
        ("Ek is lief vir New York")   Windhoek
                                        Namibia.

Namibia

Please share your thoughts with us:

Share your September 11th story. How have you been changed by the events of September 11th, or what action can you take in the spirit of Tribute to help or educate another?

World Trade Center for Ever...
and ever, and ever, and ever, and ever.....

Italy

"We wept . . . and we hugged our families."

Please share your thoughts with us:
Share your September 11th story. How have you been changed
by the events of September 11th, or what action can you take
in the spirit of Tribute to help or educate another?

I am a nurse in Boston. As we watched
the terrifying + tragic events unfred we prepared
to recieve casualties, canceled surguies, opened
beds, we sent a large Burn/Trauma team to NYC
They stayed + worked As we began to
vnderstand that there would be no more
patients coming we wept, the hospitalized
patients wept And we hugged our families
God Bless

Massachusetts

"I returned to my town with my search & rescue K9."

Please share your thoughts with us:
Share your September 11th story. How have you been changed by the events of September 11th, or what action can you take in the spirit of Tribute to help or educate another?

I Grew up in N.Y.C. HAd my Prom At the "windows of the world" my First Job AFter High school At tower 1. years lAter i moved to virginiA. on 9-11 I returned to my town with my search + rescue K9 to Find the remAins of my Fellow New yorker And Friends that i lost Here. there is not one dAy I don't think About you All

love

FAirFAX search + Resce K9

Washington, D.C.

"Nothing in this world really matters . . . except people & love!"

Please share your thoughts with us:
Share your September 11th story. How have you been changed
by the events of September 11th, or what action can you take
in the spirit of Tribute to help or educate another?

I worked at the Marriott International HQ in London
at the time. Watching the event unfold in the boardroom
TV was surreal. Visiting the centre today (2009) is
still as heart-wrenching as it was then. The bravery
of all the helpers, the love that transcended colour
or creed, the united cry for "help" and "peace", everyone
who lost someone . . . humbles me. We are only grains of
sand in the grand scheme of things. Nothing in this
world really matters . . . except people & love!

United Kingdom

Please share your thoughts with us:
Share your September 11th story. How have you been changed
by the events of September 11th, or what action can you take
in the spirit of Tribute to help or educate another?

Kia Kaha
Stand   Strong

Kia Manawanui
Be Courageous

· My thoughts are with all those who have lost
New Zealand

New Zealand

"My professor said—'This will define your generation.'"

Please share your thoughts with us:
Share your September 11th story. How have you been changed
by the events of September 11th, or what action can you take
in the spirit of Tribute to help or educate another?

As a college student in San Francisco, California, I was
sitting in sociology watching the events unfold before
me on TV. For the first few minutes I couldn't bear
to watch - I thought somehow if I didn't watch, it wouldn't
be true. My professor said - "this will define your generation.
I knew she was right → things have never been the
same. When I got back to my dorm room, my
roommate was fast asleep... I thought, "my god, she
has no idea what has happened." I turned on the
TV & watched in silence.

California

"We must learn from 9/11, so the world can avoid its repetition."

Please share your thoughts with us:
Share your September 11th story. How have you been changed by the events of September 11th, or what action can you take in the spirit of Tribute to help or educate another?

I am a history teacher. Last year my students said "what's the big deal about 9/11? In only 9 years, memory is fading?! Not on my watch! We must learn from 9/11, so the world can avoid its repetition.

Missouri

"May we never take life for granted."

Please share your thoughts with us:
Share your September 11th story. How have you been changed by the events of September 11th, or what action can you take in the spirit of Tribute to help or educate another?

I was sixteen. My uncle is a fireman in Alabama. He was injured a few weeks earlier and when I saw the fireman, all I could think about was Brian. We placed an Irondale Dept. badge here in April 2002 for "his brothers." This changed my life. I am going to be a physician in two years and I am in the military due to a commitment I made that day. May we never forget. May we never take life forgranted. May we always be watchful. Thank you for remembering.

Alabama

Please share your thoughts with us:
Share your September 11th story. How have you been changed by the events of September 11th, or what action can you take in the spirit of Tribute to help or educate another?

FÉ   FAITH

PAZ   PEACE

AMOR   LOVE

nós podemos!
We can do it!

dez/2008

Brazil

"Now it's real for him and he can heal."

Please share your thoughts with us:
Share your September 11th story. How have you been changed by the events of September 11th, or what action can you take in the spirit of Tribute to help or educate another?

My husband was killed in the attacks—WTC 2. Our children are now 7 and 5½ years old. This was their first visit to the site. When my younger son, whom I was pregnant with on 9/11/01, started bawling when he saw his father's picture (holding his older brother), I was surprised. He's never had that reaction before. Now it's real for him and he can heal.

North Carolina

"My generation . . . watched at a tender age as the world changed."

Please share your thoughts with us:
Share your September 11th story. How have you been changed by the events of September 11th, or what action can you take in the spirit of Tribute to help or educate another?

To all those who lost, not just those who lost loved ones but also those who lost hopes, dreams and aspirations. We will learn from the devastation, WE HAVE TO LEARN!
It is within the hopes, dreams and aspirations that we learn. One day a generation will stand up and make peace. It will hopefully be my generation who watched at a tender age as the world changed.

United Kingdom

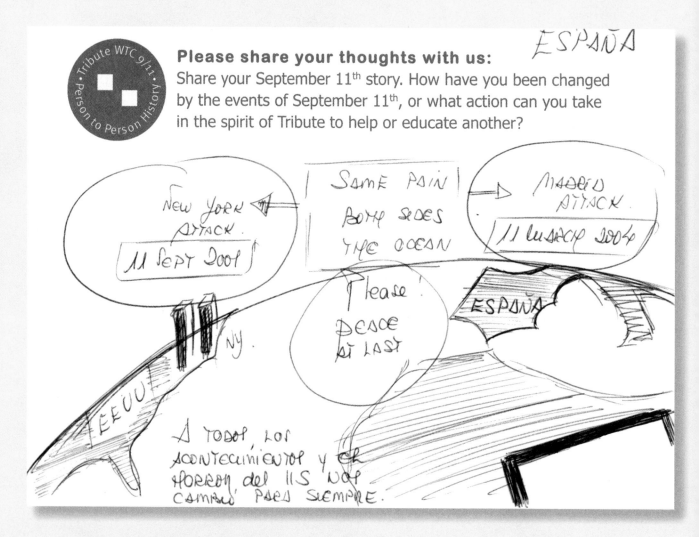

Please share your thoughts with us:

Share your September 11th story. How have you been changed by the events of September 11th, or what action can you take in the spirit of Tribute to help or educate another?

Spain

"For the first time I cry."

Please share your thoughts with us:
Share your September 11th story. How have you been changed
by the events of September 11th, or what action can you take
in the spirit of Tribute to help or educate another?

I come from a Country with a lot of Violence
(Colombia). When I lived there I Never cry
and death was a everyday thing. When
I was evacuated from the Sears Tower in
Chicago that 9/11 For the first time I cry...
I did for my now American fellows and my
Colombian people who died in the hands
of Terrorists...

Sept / 17 / 2009.

Illinois

"From now on I promise I will help my fellow friends."

Please share your thoughts with us:
Share your September 11th story. How have you been changed
by the events of September 11th, or what action can you take
in the spirit of Tribute to help or educate another?

I am one of those human beings who
selfishly have been happy in their own
small world. Today I have realised there
are so many heroes who selflessly
cared for well being of others. From now
on I promise i will help my fellow
friends in my best capacities and
this change in me, I owe to the heroes
of 9/11. I hope all souls rest inpeace.
GOD BLESS ALL.

Anonymous

Please share your thoughts with us:
Share your September 11th story. How have you been changed
by the events of September 11th, or what action can you take
in the spirit of Tribute to help or educate another?

SEPTEMBER 11, 2001 IS
THE REASON WHY I AM
A FEDERAL AIR MARSHAL.

- SEMPER FI

Washington

"And today, 7 years later, I'm just as . . . horrified."

I was 11 years old on Sept. 11, 2001. I remember sitting in my fifth grade class and my teacher standing up to make an announcement. She told us there had been an accident in New York. She didn't say what had happened. ~~crossed out~~ She didn't say people had died, the boy sitting behind me lost his sister. A friend lost her cousin and aunt, ~~crossed out~~ ~~was~~ an ~~crossed out~~ accident. And today, 7 years later, I'm just as confused about that accident as ever. Just as horrified.

New Jersey

"Each individual's stories are so precious."

Please share your thoughts with us:
Share your September 11th story. How have you been changed by the events of September 11th, or what action can you take in the spirit of Tribute to help or educate another?

The unimaginable scale of the Sept. 11 horror reminded me how each individual's stories are so precious — and can be so inspiring to others. I have devoted much of my professional time to shining light on the hopes, dreams and accomplishments of our youth.

radio producer, Los Angeles

California

"She ran, lost her shoes & she hasn't been the same after 9/11."

Please share your thoughts with us:
Share your September 11th story. How have you been changed
by the events of September 11th, or what action can you take
in the spirit of Tribute to help or educate another?

I was At work when this horrible
incident Happen - My sister worked in one of the
adjacent Buildings - (computer Data processing) to the world
Trade CenTer - I couldn't believe what happened on
that Day - I was concerned about my sister. Whether
She was Dead or Alive - Thank God she was out
she RAN, lost her Shoes & she hasn't been the same -
She AFTER 9/11 - She cut her Beautiful Long hair -
She has been Tormented With Nightmares of that horrible
Day - Bodies falling from the Buildings landing in front
of her or behind her - she went through the
Whole post traumatic stress syndrome Unable to Forget
what happened I pray for her & all the other Family of
9/11/01 victims - I pray that someday they will Find
Closure - from this horrible Event.

New York

192

Please share your thoughts with us:
Share your September 11th story. How have you been changed
by the events of September 11th, or what action can you take
in the spirit of Tribute to help or educate another?

Today
Two sisters
Came to see
Two Buildings
Two Icons
Two Planes
Too Many
Lives Ended
To Quickly

To Stay
To Go
To Remember
Forever
So Much
So Little
Too Much
and Yet
Not Enough
It's Too Much

You Remember, We Remember, They Remember, Too.

New York

"Honor the meaning this day has for thousands of Americans."

Please share your thoughts with us:
Share your September 11th story. How have you been changed by the events of September 11th, or what action can you take in the spirit of Tribute to help or educate another?

This is a day and a story that can teach anybody of any age of any nationality, and of any background. I will always remember this day and make sure that my children and grandchildren will continue to understand and honor the meaning this day has for thousands of Americans. As a first generation Chinese-American who is stereotypically torn between my two identities, this museum and this day has given me one of my most profound "proud to be American" moments. Thank you

Illinois

"We are all one!"

Please share your thoughts with us:
Share your September 11th story. How have you been changed
by the events of September 11th, or what action can you take
in the spirit of Tribute to help or educate another?

If the humanity is taken away - nothing's left.
If one person's rights are being violated...
all of us suffer!
What came out of 9/11 is sadness, and loss,
but also hope in humanity, in kindness,
in community!
We are all one!

United States

TRANSLATION

Wordless at college where I was at the moment of the tragedy, a deafening silence, closed the school, no one wanted to believe it. Professors, students, and staff held hands and cried, for the dead, but above all for those who had lost someone. Without knowing anyone I feel as though I lost lots of people, people who left home for work, or people who, like me, came to New York to visit. With this terrible attack the world shrank but humanity grew. Different peoples holding hands was something that I will never forget.

Please share your thoughts with us:
Share your September 11th story. How have you been changed by the events of September 11th, or what action can you take in the spirit of Tribute to help or educate another?

Sem palavras Na Faculdade onde estava no momento da Tragedia, um silencio ensurdeceder fedou a escola Ninguem queria acreditar. Professores, alunos e funcionarios deram as maos e choraram, pelos mortos mas sobretudo por aqueles que perderam alguem Eu sem conhecer ninguem sinto que perdi muita gente, gente que saiu de casa para trabalhar ou gente que como eu, veio a New York para visitar com este horrivel atentado o mundo ficou mais pequeno mas a humanidade ficou maior. povos diferentes de maos dadas foi algo que jamais esquecerei

Portugal

Please share your thoughts with us:
Share your September 11th story. How have you been changed by the events of September 11th, or what action can you take in the spirit of Tribute to help or educate another?

DIA DIA!

In my spoken language, that means More SOLIDARITY, HOPE, LOVE,

Cameroon

"This is one of its saddest moments."

Please share your thoughts with us:
Share your September 11th story. How have you been changed
by the events of September 11th, or what action can you take
in the spirit of Tribute to help or educate another?

In the context of the Universe
this is nothing.
In the context of time this is
nothing.

In the context of this civilisation
which we call mankind this
is one of its sadest moments.

Anonymous

"There is a solemn ambiance as you tread this ground."

Please share your thoughts with us:
Share your September 11th story. How have you been changed by the events of September 11th, or what action can you take in the spirit of Tribute to help or educate another?

Visiting the site where the Twin Towers once stood and reading about those events here at the Centre, have made me realise the horror of that day. There is a Solemn ambiance as you tread this ground, almost as if the Spirits of those that lost their lives are here, watching us, watching them.

United Kingdom

"I would spend as much time as I could with my loved ones."

Please share your thoughts with us:
Share your September 11th story. How have you been changed by the events of September 11th, or what action can you take in the spirit of Tribute to help or educate another?

I still remember the day like it was yesterday. I was in school and the next thing I knew I heard about this tragedy and my first thought was "It just can't be, it looks like a part of a movie." I didn't find out until that day my cousin worked in the WTC and with that news my heart broke, it broke for him and all the others in the buildings that day. I never got to see him as much as I liked and I promised if he came home that day I would spend more time with him. I prayed and actually had a dream that he was walking down the block one day coming home but unfortunately it stayed a dream and he NEVER came home. From that day on I promised myself that I would spend as much time as I could with my loved ones. I think about him all every day along with all the others lost in this tragedy and I send all my love to those families who lost a loved one that day. I thank all those who helped during this time. You are all heros and without everyone sticking together there would be no hope.

I love you, I miss you, and I will never forget you!

New York

TRANSLATION

When the attacks of September 11th were happening, my uncle Yuri died in Turkmenistan. I loved him very much and that's why I didn't feel what was happening in New York at that time. Today, I continue to remember the loss of my uncle and I understand the feelings of people who lost their relatives on September 11th. I hope those who lost their relatives will be okay, and we have to never forget that tragedy.

Please share your thoughts with us:

Share your September 11th story. How have you been changed by the events of September 11th, or what action can you take in the spirit of Tribute to help or educate another?

Когда это случилось, я только недавно потеряла дядю Юру, которого очень любила и трагедию 11 сентября не почувствовала так остро из-за личного горя сегодня я не могу перестать плакать и чувствую так как будто это было недавно и коснулось меня лично. Мир всем кого мы потеряли и благополучия и мира всем кто остался. Я уверена эту трагедию мир не забудет никогда.

Turkmenistan

"I pray for world peace."

Please share your thoughts with us:
Share your September 11th story. How have you been changed by the events of September 11th, or what action can you take in the spirit of Tribute to help or educate another?

In Malay,

Saya sangat terharu dengan akibat ini. Saya berdoa semoga ada aman dan damai di dunia ini.

In Jawi,

سايا سڬت ترهارو داعن أكيبت أنيٴ۔ سايا بردواٴ سموڬ أدا أمن دان داماي دي دونيا أنيٴ۔

In English,

It is a heart-moving experience towards the tragedy.
I pray for world peace.

Love, From Singapore...

Singapore

Please share your thoughts with us:
Share your September 11th story. How have you been changed
by the events of September 11th, or what action can you take
in the spirit of Tribute to help or educate another?

ON
Ne Vous pas oublie !

"we don't forget you!"

BMAI / Strasbourg - France

France

TRANSLATION

Due to the violence that took place, I believe it is our responsibility to take all precautionary measures for the future. Everyone should adopt peace, justice, and collaboration policies. Finally I wish to all humans peace, rights, and prosperous living.

From the heart to the heart,

Peace . . . from Tunisia

Please share your thoughts with us:
Share your September 11th story. How have you been changed by the events of September 11th, or what action can you take in the spirit of Tribute to help or educate another?

ما حدث من العنف ، أظن من واجبنا حميعا
اتخاذ كل الإجراءات وقايه للمستقبل .
يجب على الجميع اتخاذ سياسات سلام
وعدل وتعاون . . أتمنى في الاخير لكل
هذه الانسانيه السلام والصحة والعيش الهني .

من القلب إلى القلب
والسلام
من تونس

Tunisia

Please share your thoughts with us:
Share your September 11th story. How have you been changed
by the events of September 11th, or what action can you take
in the spirit of Tribute to help or educate another?

Saudi Arabia

Canada

"Create a better world to live!"

Please share your thoughts with us:
Share your September 11th story. How have you been changed
by the events of September 11th, or what action can you take
in the spirit of Tribute to help or educate another?

Live with Peace
Love with Care
And create a better
World
To Live! :)

India

"We cried when we heard his voice. Tears of joy for a change."

MY BROTHER, A PARAMEDIC HERE IN NYC WAS AT ONE OF THE TOWERS HELPING A BURN VICTIM WHEN THE 2ND PLANE HIT. MIRACULOUSLY, HE WAS ON THE FURTHEST SIDE AWAY FROM THE DEBRIS.

HE THEN TRANSPORTED HIS BURNED, INJURED PATIENT TO THE HOSPITAL AND SHORTLY AFTER THE TOWERS CAME DOWN.

WE DIDN'T KNOW IF HE WAS DEAD OR ALIVE FOR ALMOST 4 DAYS. WE CRIED WHEN WE HEARD HIS VOICE. TEARS OF JOY FOR A CHANGE. GOD BLESS ALL THE FAMILIES AFFECTED BY 9-11 ! WITH LOVE ALWAYS!

California

"Make the lessons of 9/11 matter daily."

Please share your thoughts with us:
Share your September 11th story. How have you been changed
by the events of September 11th, or what action can you take
in the spirit of Tribute to help or educate another?

Thanks to all those who organized, funded and
contributed to this poignant memorial to 9/11.
Thanks especially to those who visit, who read
the notes and think about the dead and bereaved,
and who hurt against the cruelty and hatred
that brought such pain. My one, only wish is
that this beautiful emotions of hope, tolerance
and camaderie can last beyond this short visit.
Make the lessons of 9/11 matter daily, and thus honor the dead.

Singapore

"It was inconceivable that we had been in the buildings a week before."

Please share your thoughts with us:
Share your September 11th story. How have you been changed by the events of September 11th, or what action can you take in the spirit of Tribute to help or educate another?

We're from Los Angeles & had been visiting NY for Labor Day '01. We went to brunch at Windows on the World for a birthday celebration & I'll never forget my young niece pointing at the planes from the windows. A week later, as we watched on TV from home, it was inconceivable that we had been in the buildings a week before. We remembered the security guards, everyone we had encountered & wondered if they were OK.

California

"We can each do little things to change the world."

Please share your thoughts with us:
Share your September 11th story. How have you been changed by the events of September 11th, or what action can you take in the spirit of Tribute to help or educate another?

I work with high school student volunteers, and I pray that if they learn nothing else, they learn that each individual is responsible for the continuation of peace through an active pursuit of understanding and tolerance of every human being. Alone, we can each do little things to change the world and together we can absolutely change the world To honor all those who sacrificed on 9/11, we each need to ask ourselves what difference can I make and then act to make a difference Peace to all —

Green Bay, WI

Wisconsin

After I visited the September 11th ground zero center, I felt that what happened in NY could happen anywhere in the world. Therefore, we need to teach our children that violence has to be fought and that everyone should keep remembering freedom. Thus we need to fight terrorists and terminate violence, and always raise the motto: no to violence, no to terrorism, yes to freedom, yes to democracy.

Please share your thoughts with us: (ARABIK)

Share your September 11th story. How have you been changed by the events of September 11th, or what action can you take in the spirit of Tribute to help or educate another?

بعد زيارتي لمقر أو لمركز أحداث السبتمبر أحسست أن ما جرى لمي نيويورك
قد يجري أو يحدث في أي مكان في العالم، ولذا علينا أن نعلم أُطفالنا
على أن العنف يجب أن يحارب وعلى الجميع أن يتذكر الحرية،
ومن هنا علينا أن نحارب ونقاتل الارهابيين من أن ننهي العنف
ونرفع دائماً شعار لا للعنف ولارهاب، نعم للحرية والديمقراطية

حيائي براهي

١١/ ٥/ ٢٠٠٨

Iraq

"The hole in my heart is still there. . . ."

Please share your thoughts with us:
Share your September 11th story. How have you been changed by the events of September 11th, or what action can you take in the spirit of Tribute to help or educate another?

EVERYONE ON THIS WORLD KNOWS WHERE HE OR SHE HAD BEEN AT THE TIME THESE ATTACKS HAPPENED. I'VE BEEN AT HOME IN BERLIN, GERMANY. SOME OF MY BEST FRIENDS WERE ON VACATION IN NY. UNFORTUNATELY THE'VE CHOSEN 9,11 TO VISIT WTC. ONE OF THREE GUYS SURVIVED, THE OTHER TWO WERE NEVER FOUND. BEING HERE AT THE TRIBUTE CENTER TODAY IS REALLY HARD. IT GOT TO FIGHT TO KEEP BACK MY TEARS, BECAUSE THE HOLE IN MY HEART IS STILL THERE...
LET US ALL JUST PRAY AND DO OUR BEST THAT SUCH A THING WON'T HAPPEN AGAIN.

GERMANY

Germany

"'Ahimsa' [nonviolence] is the only way forward for mankind."

Please share your thoughts with us:
Share your September 11th story. How have you been changed by the events of September 11th, or what action can you take in the spirit of Tribute to help or educate another?

Our thoughts goes out to the all the victims of mindless violence all over the world. Spreading the message of peace "AHIMSA" is the only way forward for mankind.

India

"To send their thoughts to those who really needed it."

Please share your thoughts with us:
Share your September 11th story. How have you been changed
by the events of September 11th, or what action can you take
in the spirit of Tribute to help or educate another?

September 11, 2001 was my 15th birthday
and I will never forget watching the footage
and classmates telling me they were, "so
sorry my birthday was ruined" I remember
repeatedly telling them to not feel sorry for
me and instead to send their thoughts to those
who really needed it, those who lost their lives, the
family members, the NYPD, the NYFD & the volunteers.

Wisconsin

Please share your thoughts with us:
Share your September 11th story. How have you been changed by the events of September 11th, or what action can you take in the spirit of Tribute to help or educate another?

Illinois

"The events of 9/11 marked my life forever."

Please share your thoughts with us:
Share your September 11th story. How have you been changed by the events of September 11th, or what action can you take in the spirit of Tribute to help or educate another?

The events of 9/11 not only affected people in the USA but all over the world. Living in the Dominican Republic at the time we felt the impact of what happened and felt a sense of unity to our American neighbors. It changed my appreciation of love, devotion, service, dedication, and unity that can come together for a nation, and a world, in need. The events of 9/11 marked my life forever, and I will never forget ♡

Dominican Republic

Dominican Republic

Please share your thoughts with us:
Share your September 11th story. How have you been changed by the events of September 11th, or what action can you take in the spirit of Tribute to help or educate another?

Tibet

On September 11th 2001, I had my baby with me on my lap and I could barely believe what I saw, what I saw "live" on television. I held my daughter tight, really tight, so tight I squeezed her. She was next to me. How many people lost their children on this day?

Please share your thoughts with us:
Share your September 11th story. How have you been changed by the events of September 11th, or what action can you take in the spirit of Tribute to help or educate another?

Am 11 Sept 2001 hatte ich mein Baby bei mir auf dem Schoß sitzen, und konnte kaum glauben, was ich da im Fernsehe „live" sah Ich hielt meine Tochte ganz fest bei mir. Ich drückte sie Sie war bei mir Wieviele haben Ihre Kinde an diesem Tag verloren '?!

Germany

"My son served to protect his country."

Please share your thoughts with us:
Share your September 11th story. How have you been changed
by the events of September 11th, or what action can you take
in the spirit of Tribute to help or educate another?

It took me nine years to come here and
visit. I was at the center on Memorial Day weekend
I was presented with a flag that was flown in
honor of my son here at hollow ground. My son
served to protect his country. I also lost
a friend on one of the planes that hit the tower.
I come here to pay my respect to all who died
and also to give my respect for my son.

KiA 11/27/07

New York

"The day that a divided nation united."

Please share your thoughts with us:
Share your September 11th story. How have you been changed
by the events of September 11th, or what action can you take
in the spirit of Tribute to help or educate another?

NEVER HAVE THE VIOLENT ACTIONS OF SO FEW AFFECTED SO MANY
11TH SEPTEMBER 2001 WAS THE DAY THAT A DIVIDED NATION
UNITED. THE OCEANS OF THE WORLD AND THE VAST DISTANCES
WERE NARROWED AND A SPIRIT OF BROTHERHOOD, TOGETHERNESS
AND LOVE TRANSLATED + TRANSCENDED EVERYTHING.

EVERY LAST SOUL FOREVER REMEMBERED

MANCHESTER, ENGLAND

United Kingdom

Italy

"It certainly has defined our generation."

Please share your thoughts with us:
Share your September 11th story. How have you been changed
by the events of September 11th, or what action can you take
in the spirit of Tribute to help or educate another?

I was 16 and had just been hanging out with my first boyfriend after school when my mum picked me up in the car and told me what happened. We read the newspapers in the sixth form common room at school every day for the next few weeks, the ensuing events woke us up to world politics. It certainly has defined our generation. We took strength from America's courage when London was attacked a few years later – when my fellow university students were moving to the city for internships and the reality of terrorism was brought to our doorstep. It has all shaped our perspective on the world, on politics, on how we travel, how we view others. We will not forget! From England 24th Jun '09

United Kingdom

"Teach children to be open to all people."

Please share your thoughts with us:
Share your September 11th story. How have you been changed by the events of September 11th, or what action can you take in the spirit of Tribute to help or educate another?

I was teaching my Learning Support class of 3rd graders in a school north of Pittsburgh, PA when a fellow teacher came in whispering to me about the attack. We watched and watched as all unfolded on the news of N.Y, WASH D.C. & closer to home Flight 93 in Somerset, PA.

My goal was, and was even greater since this event, to teach children to be open to all people regardless of religion, color or ethnicity. I pray we can achieve that someday.

Pgh, PA

Pennsylvania

"We are all one people."

Please share your thoughts with us:
Share your September 11th story. How have you been changed by the events of September 11th, or what action can you take in the spirit of Tribute to help or educate another?

I am an Irish pilot working in the Gulf. I sit beside my arab co-pilots every day. They are wonderful, wonderful friends. On Sept 11th they were shocked, horrified and a little bit shamed. They should not have been. We are all one people. It is only a minority on all sides that let us down. Dia Duit; Asalam alakum (God be with you)

Ireland

"Since then I do everything with and only with love."

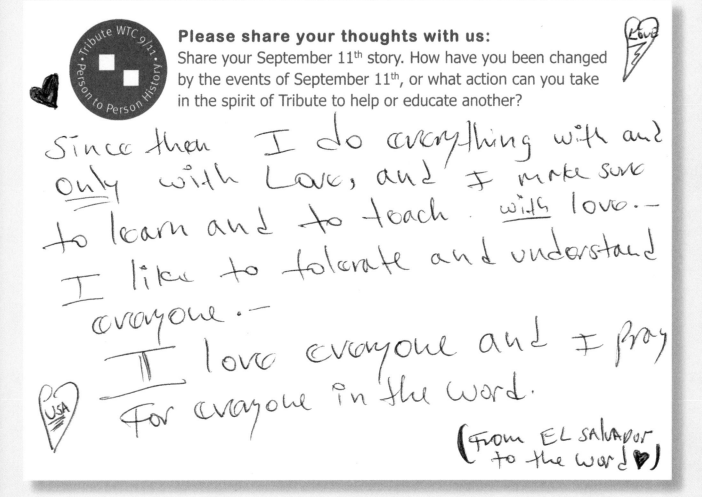

Please share your thoughts with us:
Share your September 11th story. How have you been changed by the events of September 11th, or what action can you take in the spirit of Tribute to help or educate another?

Since then I do everything with and only with Love, and I make sure to learn and to teach. with love. — I like to tolerate and understand everyone. —
I love everyone and I pray for everyone in the word.
(From EL SALVADOR to the word ♥)

El Salvador

"There is a common human bond."

Please share your thoughts with us:
Share your September 11th story. How have you been changed
by the events of September 11th, or what action can you take
in the spirit of Tribute to help or educate another?

I was in Los Angeles, getting ready for work
when the news broke that the first tower had been
hit. At work, we saw the second tower being hit on
television. Our world was changed forever. This is
my fourth visit to the WTC site - twice alone, once
with family, and once with friends. The emotion of
each visit is the same. There is such an overwhelming
sense of loss and sadness. Yet, here in 2008, seeing
hundreds of people here from all over the nation and
world visiting this place there is a common human
bond. We all grieve for those who perished, their
families, and pray that peace will ultimately
come to us all . . . .

8-10-08

Virginia

Please share your thoughts with us:

Share your September 11th story. How have you been changed by the events of September 11th, or what action can you take in the spirit of Tribute to help or educate another?

Japan

"How religion & politics could inflict so much pain."

Please share your thoughts with us:
Share your September 11th story. How have you been changed by the events of September 11th, or what action can you take in the spirit of Tribute to help or educate another?

My parents woke me in the early hours of the morning at home in New Zealand. The first plane had just hit the North Tower and it was being re-played on our news. I remember being speechless, my heart went out to all the people on the floors who were killed + injured. As further events occurred I was dumbfounded at how religion + politics could inflict so much pain. Everyone I met that day had a quietness about them - a sadness. This gallery is an amazing record of events and a testament to the Fire Dept, Police Dept + all of those who helped + supported NYC after this tragedy. I will share what I've seen here back home in NZ - Hope.!!

New Zealand

Tribute WTC 9/11 · Person to Person History

Please share your thoughts with us:
Share your September 11th story. How have you been changed
by the events of September 11th, or what action can you take
in the spirit of Tribute to help or educate another?

We spread
- Love
- Peace
- Friendship
- Humanity

LOVE ∘ PAKISTAN ∘

Pakistan

231

"Compassion, kindness . . . love."

Tribute WTC 9/11 • Person to Person History •

Please share your thoughts with us:
Share your September 11th story. How have you been changed by the events of September 11th, or what action can you take in the spirit of Tribute to help or educate another?

9-11-2010

It is impossible to put into words how my brothers murder, witnessed by one third of the worlds population, has change my life. It is a saddness, a unique type of grief that I will never understand but have learned to partner with it for the rest of my life. Compassion, Kindness, ... love.

Anonymous

Please share your thoughts with us:

Share your September 11th story. How have you been changed by the events of September 11th, or what action can you take in the spirit of Tribute to help or educate another?

11
Sept

Nevicherà per Sempre sul gelo di
NYC

with love

Italy

"To all who worked so hard to save life."

Please share your thoughts with us:
Share your September 11th story. How have you been changed
by the events of September 11th, or what action can you take
in the spirit of Tribute to help or educate another?

The first thing we had to do on our first trip to New York from the UK was to pay tribute — to those who lost their lives, to all who worked so hard to save life, heal and comfort — and to rededicate ourselves to live and work every day promoting, in whatever ways we can, peace between all nations

United Kingdom

Please share your thoughts with us:
Share your September 11th story. How have you been changed
by the events of September 11th, or what action can you take
in the spirit of Tribute to help or educate another?

No MORE WARS!!!
ONLY LOVE & PEACE !!!
LET'S LOVE EACH OTHER
No MORE WHITE BLACK YELLOW etc
WE ARE ALL IN ONE BIG FAMILY !!!
2008

China

Please share your thoughts with us: <u>9/11/09</u>

Share your September 11th story. How have you been changed by the events of September 11th, or what action can you take in the spirit of Tribute to help or educate another?

IT HAS BEEN 8 YEARS —

AS YEARS PASS —
AND FAMILIES GROW.
AND CHILDREN LAUGH
WE ALWAYS KNOW
A HAND, A HEART ♡
YOUR LOVE WE KNOW
IT LIGHTS OUR PATH
TO WHERE WE GO!
WE WILL NEVER FORGET YOU, KEVIN!

FOR KEVIN

LOST TO US ON 9/11/01 IN TOWER II

New York

Please share your thoughts with us:
Share your September 11th story. How have you been changed
by the events of September 11th, or what action can you take
in the spirit of Tribute to help or educate another?

We will never forget
that day for the horror
it caused and brother
and sisterhood it created
for us all. With love
from CANADA.

Canada

"Something good has come of that dreadful day."

Please share your thoughts with us:

Share your September 11th story. How have you been changed by the events of September 11th, or what action can you take in the spirit of Tribute to help or educate another?

On September 11th I was teaching my year 7 class German, we were learning words for family members. I taught the words for Mutti, Vati, Bruder and Schwester and used the Simpson's family, I used Bart and his family as so many of my students have broken homes and difficult family situations.

Today I am sitting here in New York with my class of year 10 students. I am so proud of the way they have responded to Tribute WTC. They have shown horror, repulsion, distress and love for each other as we have walked around. If our future is in their hands then something good has come of that dreadful day. They will do everything possible to prevent something like this happening again. They have given me comfort and hope. For you too, New York, this is comfort and hope.

x.

United Kingdom

HOPE

When the power of Love overcomes the Lo... of power, the wor... will know Peace

Remembering yesterday...
Hoping for tomorrow...

HOPE

"Peace in the Middle East."

Please share your thoughts with us:
Share your September 11th story. How have you been changed
by the events of September 11th, or what action can you take
in the spirit of Tribute to help or educate another?

In where I come from there were a lot of terorist actions. Though,
It's important to distinguish between the terorist individuals
and the people in the countries where they came from.
Big majority of Pallestinians want to live in peace and quite as Afgans
or any other mouslim.
In 9/11, I was in my duty service in the Israeli Army, fighting in Gaza
against terorists. Last year I was studying Environmental science in
the Arava Institute in Israel, together with Pallestinians and Jordanian
I truely hope that by the time the Freedom Tower will be
accomplished, there will be a peace in the middle East.

Israel

"A city mourns. A city will rebuild."

- I was in my final high school year when the plane struck – I had no idea

- We talked about it in class – I had no idea

- I studied protest, war and terror including September 11 – I still had no idea

- Today, at this tribute centre, my hands shake, my eyes well, and only now do I walk past the walls and begin to understand A city mourns A city will rebuild

Australia

Please share your thoughts with us:

Share your September 11th story. How have you been changed by the events of September 11th, or what action can you take in the spirit of Tribute to help or educate another?

Anonymous

Please share your thoughts with us:
Share your September 11th story. How have you been changed by the events of September 11th, or what action can you take in the spirit of Tribute to help or educate another?

Acknowledgments

Thank you to the Board of Directors of the September 11th Families' Association: Howard Cash, Beth Dannhauser, Tom Fontana, Billy Goldfeder, Richard Kennedy, Larry Levy, Cristyne Nicholas, Dan Nigro, Marc Silberberg, and Dennis Smith for your leadership, support, and enthusiasm. The book has been made possible by Jennifer Adams for her idea, inspiration, and total commitment to creating the Tribute WTC Visitor Center from the ground up and ensuring it thrives. Many on our staff have played a role in putting the book together. I would like to thank Wendy Aibel-weiss for her creative direction of the Tribute Center and for originating the idea of placing the visitor cards in the Tribute Center. I am grateful to our curator Meriam Lobel, with whom I have been reading and appreciating these cards over these past five years, for her initiative and devotion to choosing a broad selection of individual messages to be published in a book. Caroline Bevan has been a masterful manager of the card collection and prepared them for publication. Josie Chiles has provided guidance and enthusiasm. Thank you to Josephine Brune who for the past two years has volunteered her time lovingly reading and organizing the cards. I sincerely appreciate the dedication and expertise of the lawyers at Weil, Gotshal & Manges LLP, the team at Christopher Little Literary Agency, and everyone at Globe Pequot Press, especially Lara Asher. A very special thank you to our remarkable 9/11 community volunteers whose willingness to share their stories make the experience at the Tribute Center a meaningful personal exchange.

About the Tribute WTC Visitor Center

The Tribute WTC Visitor Center is located at 120 Liberty Street in New York City along the south side of the World Trade Center site. The Tribute Center was created by the September 11th Families' Association, a section 501(c)3 non-profit corporation, to support and share the personal stories of victims, survivors, rescue and recovery workers, residents of Lower Manhattan, and volunteers who responded to help in the recovery. Today, volunteers representing all of these constituencies share their stories daily with visitors to the Tribute Center and on walking tours of the World Trade Center site. Volunteers share the authentic experiences of those most affected by the events of February 26, 1993, and September 11, 2001. In the Tribute Center, visitors experience person-to-person accounts through videos, audios, and printed quotations. The stories recount the dynamism of the World Trade Center community prior to September 11, 2001, the day of the attacks, the nine months of recovery, and a poignant memorial to the victims where photographs contributed by their families are displayed. The Tribute Center concludes by offering visitors a place to engage in dialogue about 9/11 and share their own feelings and thoughts about the future on visitor cards.

The Tribute Center conveys the courage, grief, and heroism of those who responded to the tragedy and the steps taken towards working for a more peaceful world by many of those impacted by the events. The Tribute Center welcomes visitors seven days a week. Please visit our website for details: www.tributewtc.org. The Tribute Center's educational materials for young people emphasize the humanity and compassion that arose in response to the acts of terrorism on September 11, 2001: www.tributewtc.org/programs/toolkit.html.

About Lee Ielpi

Lee Ielpi volunteered with his local Great Neck Vigilant Fire Department. He spent his career as a firefighter with the New York City Fire Department serving as a member of Rescue 2. Since losing his son Jonathan Lee Ielpi, Squad 288, FDNY, at the World Trade Center, Lee has dedicated himself to responding to the attacks on the World Trade Center with an eye towards making tomorrow a better day. He joined with the September 11th Families' Association in November 2001 to represent the interests of the 9/11 community. Lee has served on the Board of Directors since 2002 and has served as the Board President since 2007. In 2004, Lee along with Jennifer Adams cofounded the Tribute WTC Visitor Center. Lee is a native of Great Neck, New York. He is a father of two girls, Anne Marie and Melissa, and two boys, Jonathan and Brendan, and grandfather of seven grandchildren.

t in silent horror • We are changed forever • We will never forget • HOPE • I can see the

et • SPERANZA • Stand strong Be courageous • Peace to the victims Respect to the famili

I do • Never again not in any country • Last time I was in New York I stood on top of the

derful children • From that day on I promised myself that I would spend as much time as

y • To this day that phone call will haunt me • The events of 9/11 marked my life forever

olutely change the world • A day that changed the world • Let us teach compassion and c

ove from everyone was tremendous to see • HOPE • Every time I think of that day my hea

ce then I do everything with and only with love • From now on I promise I will help my fel

nd effect on me • Celebrate life and be grateful for everything we have • I'll never forget t

e forgiveness • This was America's worst and best hour • A city mourns A city will rebuild

r service • To my Brothers on FDNY you are the best of the best without a doubt • Where

time • We are all one • On September 11th 2001 all state lines became erased • Peace h

ld never forget • Steel is not the greatest metal in the world the human spirit is • PACE •

nt brought out the best in people • I believe that there is a lot of good in humanity • We al

kes every inch of me even today • Peace starts from within • I have become more aware of

everyone reacted is our legacy • The twin towers symbolized the hope of world peace • S

epeated • PAIX • May we never take life for granted • LA PAZ • I sat in silent horror • We

behind • LA PAZ • We are changed forever • We will never forget • SPERANZA • Stand s

listening • The world is one village one family • Why? • What can I do • Never again not

ore them and pray • His hopes and dreams live on in his two wonderful children • From th

e in my heart is still there • Make the lessons of 9/11 matter daily • To this day that phon

can do little things to change the world and together we can absolutely change the world

should be together to bear such awful grief • But the spirit of love from everyone was trer

the entire world • I remember how beautiful the sky was • Since then I do everything with

granted • The silence from their lost lives has had a profound effect on me • Celebrate lif

h stored in my head reminding me to live each day and to have forgiveness • This was Am

unified • Peace love joy for all countries • Thank you for your service • To my Brothers

n • Little did I know the towers would be gone in my lifetime • We are all one • On Septe

as in that moment that I became an adult • May the world never forget • Steel is not the g

onsibility and awareness as a global citizen • This event brought out the best in people •

one people • PAIX • What happened on September 11 shakes every inch of me even today

ent • What happened here in our country was a tragedy How everyone reacted is our lega